Raising
Drug-Free
Kids

Raising
Drug-Free
Kids

100 Tips
for Parents

ALETHA SOLTER, PH.D.

Da Capo
LIFE
LONG

Da Capo Lifelong Books
A Member of the Perseus Books Group

This book is an educational resource focusing on parenting practices, which can help to prevent drug abuse in children, teenagers, and young adults. It is not intended to be a substitute for medical or psychological advice or treatment. Many of the behaviors and symptoms mentioned in this book can be an indication of serious emotional or physical problems. Parents are advised to consult with a competent physician or psychologist whenever their children display behavioral, emotional, or physical problems of any kind. Children's behavior is the result of many complex factors. The author does not guarantee that the advice in this book will prevent drug use, abuse, or addiction in children, teenagers, or adults. Additionally, the author shall have neither liability nor responsibility to any person or entity with respect to any damage caused, or alleged to be caused, directly or indirectly by the information contained in this book.

Designed by Brent Wilcox
Set in 11 point Fairfield Light by the Perseus Books Group

Library of Congress Cataloging-in-Publication Data
Solter, Aletha Jauch, 1945–
    Raising drug-free kids : 100 tips for parents / Aletha Solter.
       p.   cm.
    Includes bibliographical references.
    ISBN-13: 978-0-7382-1074-2 (pbk. : alk. paper)
    ISBN-10: 0-7382-1074-9 (pbk. : alk. paper)
    1. Children—Drug use.   2. Drug abuse—Prevention.   3. Parenting.   I. Title.
    HV5824.C45S65   2006
    649'.48--dc22

                                                                    2006018950

Published by Da Capo Press
A Member of the Perseus Books Group
http://www.dacapopress.com

Da Capo Press books are available at special discounts for bulk purchases in the U.S. by corporations, institutions, and other organizations. For more information, please contact the Special Markets Department at the Perseus Books Group, 11 Cambridge Center, Cambridge, MA 02142, or call (800) 255-1514 or (617) 252-5298, or e-mail special.markets@perseusbooks.com.

1 2 3 4 5 6 7 8 9—09 08 07 06

Contents

Introduction

We live in a drug-crazy world. If you are a parent worried about how to protect your child from drugs, you are not alone. Many parents are deeply concerned about substance abuse in young people and don't know what they can do to prevent it. Most books about raising drug-free children begin with the preteen or teenage years. But there is much that you can do long before your children reach those notorious teenage years. This book will give you tips from birth to adulthood for raising a drug-free child. You will find useful ideas in it whether your child is an infant, a five-year-old, a fifteen-year-old, or a young adult.

I have assembled the most relevant and current information available on child development and adolescent substance abuse to provide you with concrete advice for inoculating your child against the temptations of drugs. Many of you may be reading this book long after your children's births and are perhaps wondering how your children will turn out if you have not followed all of these tips when they were younger. Rest assured that failure to follow these tips does not imply that your children will become drug addicts! Furthermore, even if you have not raised your children according to the suggestions for the early years, it is never too late to begin making changes that will help your children resist drugs.

Even with the best of parenting, there is no guarantee that your child will never smoke a cigarette or try marijuana. If your child has experimented with drugs, don't despair. Given the resources and information you had when your child was younger, you have done your best. Furthermore, you are not the only influence on your child. Movies, television, popular music, the Internet, sports heroes, and your child's friends all have a powerful influence on your child, so don't blame yourself if your child has tried drugs.

If your child is already dependent on drugs, and his or her life is spiraling out of control, you will need expert support and guidance that is beyond the scope of this book. Addiction is an illness that does not go away by itself. Although the suggestions in this book will still be helpful in improving your relationship with your child, it will be very difficult to get your child off drugs without professional treatment. (See Resources for suggestions on where to get help.) After your child has been through treatment, this book can be a parenting resource for you while you help your child build a new life free of drugs.

When I was a graduate student in psychology in the early 1970s, I lived for five years in the upstairs apartment of an old farmhouse in California. There were "hippies" living in the other three apartments in the house, who frequently smoked marijuana. They also occasionally used other illegal drugs, such as LSD and "speed" (amphetamine). I once observed them carefully weighing small plastic bags of white powder, and I knew it wasn't sugar! One of the young men built a greenhouse in the backyard where he grew marijuana plants. We shared a large backyard and front patio and interacted frequently. These young people, who came from middle-class and affluent families, felt the need to rebel against the "establishment," which they saw as violent (this was during the Vietnam War), hypocritical, and overly focused on material wealth.

I had university classes to attend, papers to write, and exams to pass, and I did not want to mess with the chemistry of my brain. So I politely refused whenever a joint was passed around, and to their credit, the other young people respected my choice. When the marijuana smoke drifted up through my living room window in the summer, I would simply close the window. I am telling this story not to brag about my abstinence but to convey my conviction that the availability of drugs is only a small part of the drug problem and that it is possible to resist drugs even when they are readily available.

Efforts to curb the drug problem among youth through law enforcement efforts are like trying to empty water out of a leaky boat. As long as the boat continues to leak, there will be a continuous need to keep it afloat by emptying out the water. The goal should be to fix the boat. Instead of constantly fighting the flow of drugs into our neighborhoods, we should also be focusing on ways to decrease the *desire* for drugs. Although law enforcement is important, it cannot, by itself, solve the drug problems of our youth.

Furthermore, illegal drugs are only a small part of the problem. There are probably legal psychoactive substances in your bathroom cabinet (such as cough syrup, tranquilizers, or opiate-based painkillers). Your home or office probably also contains some products (such as glue or hair spray) that kids could use as inhalants. The most dangerous and lethal drugs are tobacco (nicotine) and alcohol, both of which are legal for adults and readily available to young people. These two drugs cause more deaths than all the other drugs combined. Preventive parenting is therefore the only way to curb the drug problem at its source.

The approach described in this book may be quite different from other parenting advice you have heard. Many books suggest that children need more "discipline," meaning that parents should punish their children for breaking rules. However, strict authoritarian control often backfires by causing children to rebel. Although some children may benefit from more consistency and structure (but not punishment), *the root cause of most behavioral problems, including substance abuse, is not a lack of discipline but rather a lack of connection.* Children who lack a close relationship with at least one loving parent are at risk for substance abuse, no matter how much "discipline" you impose on them. Likewise, children who have a close relationship with a loving parent are more likely to resist drugs.

The one hundred tips in this book will show you how to establish and maintain a close connection to your child at each stage of your child's development. It is never too late to improve your relationship with your child. At the root of this approach is spending time with your child, using a nonpunitive approach to discipline, and accepting your child's emotions. Another important aspect of drug resistance is learning about the various drugs, their effects, and their dangers, so I have also included many tips about how to give drug-related information to children at different ages.

I have organized the chapters according to age so you can easily find the tips that are most relevant to you. However, because many of the tips for younger children also apply to older ones, I recommend that you also read the tips for younger children, especially the chapter immediately preceding the age of your child.

My three other books describe a complete approach to non-punitive parenting (called Aware Parenting). I have lectured in eleven countries and done consultations with parents for more than twenty years. My husband and I have raised a son and a daughter using this approach, and I am proud to say that neither of them smokes or abuses alcohol or drugs. They never had any desire to experiment with drugs or alcohol, even though they attended public schools where drugs were easily available and a university where alcohol consumption was rampant.

You will find that keeping your children off drugs is not the only positive outcome of this approach. In addition to becoming drug resistant, your children will grow up to be emotionally healthy, intellectually competent, cooperative, nonviolent, and compassionate and will become autonomous without the need to rebel during adolescence. My wish for you and for all parents is that your children will reach their highest potential and that you will enjoy a close, lifelong relationship with them, unhampered by substance abuse and addiction.

Chapter 1

The Basics

Tip 1

Help your child feel connected.

Research studies have shown that adolescents who feel more connected to their families and schools are emotionally healthier, less violent, and less likely to use drugs. It is therefore vitally important to establish a close, loving relationship with each of your children, beginning in infancy and continuing into adulthood.

The connection between a parent and child is like a rubber bungee cord. Sometimes the cord will be very short, such as when your child is a toddler and wants to climb into your lap. Sometimes the bungee cord will be very long and stretched, such as when your teen leaves home to attend college. Or it will be stretched symbolically, as when one of you is very angry at the other. But your children need to know that the cord will always be there as a symbolic representation of a strong connection to you. They need the reassurance that, no matter how far away they are, and no matter how angry either of you feels, the bond between you will never break.

Children also need to feel connected to their family. You can accomplish this by doing activities together as a family, such as playing, eating, working on projects at home, traveling, singing, dancing, and simply talking together. This feeling of belonging to a family and a home is every child's birthright, without which a child is like a ship without a rudder. If your family has experienced changes through death, separation, divorce, remarriage, or frequent moves, your children have an even greater need to feel that they belong to a family, no matter how small or diverse it is.

Finally, children benefit from belonging to a community, whether it's a neighborhood, a religious group, or an extended family of aunts, uncles, and cousins. Communities offer security, companionship, and mutual aid in times of need. If there is a rupture in your bond with your children because of anger, separation, divorce, illness, or death, your children need to know that there are other adults who care about them, adults they can turn to for help and emotional support.

Throughout this book you will find tips for specific ways you can strengthen your child's bond to you, your family, and a community of other caring families. This network of emotional connections is at the root of drug-resistant parenting. If your relationship with your child is strained, realize that it is never too late to repair it.

With a strong connection to you, your children will be more likely to want to please you and to adopt your value system as their own. With a strong connection to a family and a community of caring adults, your children will have a place to call home and a network of support as they grow in autonomy and venture out into the world.

Tip 2

Realize that genetics is not destiny.

There is evidence that the tendency to crave alcohol and become dependent on it is a genetic trait, and you will probably know if this inherited trait runs in your family. If your child is adopted, it would be useful for you to know if his parents or other relatives were alcoholics. There is also evidence that susceptibility to nicotine addiction (tobacco) is inherited.

In addition to these specific genetic factors, there is a more general inherited trait, which predisposes people to engage in addictive behaviors. This temperament trait involves what psychologists call "externalizing" behaviors. People with this temperament are more likely to be impulsive and oppositional and are more likely to engage in risky behavior. People with "internalizing" behaviors are more likely to be cautious, anxious, and inhibited.

These two opposite traits are similar to another research-based categorization, which distinguishes less sensitive people (the externalizers) from those who are highly sensitive (the internalizers). About 15 to 20 percent of people are highly sensitive, and this appears to be hereditary.

If your child is highly sensitive by nature, he will be less likely to experiment with drugs because he will find them overstimulating, especially stimulants and hallucinogens. (He will probably also avoid wild parties.) However, the inherited trait of high sensitivity will not entirely protect your child from the dangers of alcohol or drugs, because highly sensitive, shy people are vulnerable to binge drinking in social situations. What seems to happen is that they take a first drink to relax because they feel awkward and shy. After the first drink they lose some of their inhibitions, including the natural inhibition to use alcohol, and so they continue to drink but don't know when to stop. Afterward they feel deeply ashamed and remorseful. This is a different pattern of drinking from the steady drinking of typical alcoholics, but it can be just as damaging and dangerous.

Obviously, you cannot change your child's genes. Rest assured, however, that if your child has inherited a genetic predisposition for alcohol or nicotine, or if he is an impulsive risk taker, he will *not* automatically grow up to become an alcoholic or a drug addict. If your child is highly sensitive, he will *not* automatically become a binge drinker in social situations. Although these genetic factors can play a role in later substance abuse, studies have shown that *social and environmental factors (including parenting practices) have a much greater influence.*

Numerous studies have shown that nonpunitive approaches to discipline reduce the likelihood of substance abuse during adolescence. You can further decrease your child's risk by providing him with love, attention, stability, information, support, and good role models. The tips in this book will help you raise your child to be drug free, whatever genes he has inherited.

Tip 3

Don't give your child alcohol or drugs.

If you want your children to be drug free as adults, it makes sense to avoid giving them drugs while they are growing up. This advice may sound obvious. However, some people are unaware of all the ways in which children can be exposed to drugs.

Secondhand smoke can have the same physiological effects as direct inhalation of smoke, so if you and your children are in the presence of a person who smokes tobacco or marijuana, try to protect them from exposure. Open a window, politely ask the person to stop smoking, or leave the room.

It is also important to avoid giving your children sips of alcohol. Although it may be tempting to let them taste your wine or beer, this practice undermines your message that alcohol is dangerous for growing bodies. Most children dislike the taste of alcohol at first, but they can learn to like it. It is especially risky to let your child taste alcohol if she has inherited a genetic predisposition for alcohol addiction.

Also, avoid involving your children in your use of drugs or alcohol. Fetching your own can of beer, instead of asking your child to get it, reinforces your message that alcohol is not for children. (See Tip 89 for the reasons why alcohol and drugs are more dangerous for children than for adults.)

Jokes about people getting drunk or high expose children symbolically to alcohol or drugs. These jokes are not funny, and they make light of a serious problem. They can desensitize children to the danger of alcohol or drug abuse.

Caffeine is not as dangerous as some other drugs, but it is wise to limit your children's caffeine intake. This stimulant is in coffee, tea, chocolate, and numerous soft drinks. Frequent consumption of caffeine during childhood may predispose your children to want more stimulants later on. Furthermore, caffeine can cause hyperactivity, insomnia, and constipation.

This tip would be incomplete without mentioning the prescription medications we give children to control their behavior. This practice is common in the United States and is spreading to other countries. When we give children stimulants or other medication with a direct effect on the brain (psychoactive drugs), we teach them that it's acceptable to consume chemical substances in order to alter behavior or feel better. This contradicts the lesson we want them to learn about drugs. Many medications for children's behavioral problems are addictive, and they are increasingly being abused by adolescents. (See Tip 40.) If we want to raise drug-free children, we need to question the practice of routinely giving them psychoactive drugs and look for alternative ways to help them with emotional or behavioral problems.

A word of caution: If you plan to withdraw your child from psychoactive medication, be sure to do so under close medical supervision.

Tip 4

Get treatment if you abuse alcohol or drugs.

Children with an addicted parent are at increased risk for substance abuse. Although some of this risk is the result of an inherited predisposition, much of it is also environmental. It would be both hypocritical and unrealistic for you to expect your children to avoid drugs if you yourself consume these substances irresponsibly. You owe it to yourself and your children to stop abusing alcohol or drugs.

There are now many treatments and recovery methods to choose from, both medical and nonmedical. Many people have benefited from the spiritual approach advocated by Alcoholics Anonymous (AA) and Narcotics Anonymous (NA), while others prefer the nonspiritual support offered by Secular Organizations for Sobriety (SOS International). Whatever method you choose, it is wise to have close medical supervision and a supportive network of caring people. During the withdrawal process, you may feel painful emotions as well as very uncomfortable, even life-threatening, physical symptoms. It will take time for your brain to function normally after withdrawal. Relapses are common, so don't be too hard on yourself and don't give up. Realize that the only workable solution for you may be total abstinence, and try to develop relationships with people who are sober and drug free.

If you have not yet overcome your addiction, be honest with your children, because it will be difficult to hide it from them. Children, especially teens, are quick to spot inconsistent or hypocritical behavior. Tell them that you have a problem and that you are working on it. Explain that you thought you could stop drinking or using the drug any time but discovered that you couldn't stop once you had become addicted. Let them know what you are doing to overcome your addiction. Your children will respect you for your honesty. However, you will lose their respect if you do not follow through with your intention to become sober and drug free.

If you are drug free but have a partner who abuses alcohol or drugs, your family situation will be unhealthy for your children. You may be facilitating (enabling) your partner's addiction without realizing it. Changing your own behavior and your response to your partner may be the trigger that will help him understand that he has a problem and needs help. You will need a lot of support as you work toward a healthier family situation, whatever the outcome. Seek support to understand the nature of addiction, learn what you can do to help your partner give up alcohol or drugs, and find ways to build a healthy, fulfilling life for yourself. (See the Resources section for sources of support.)

Tip 5

Get support if you are the child of an alcoholic.

If one or both of your parents was an alcoholic when you were growing up, then you will face special challenges as a parent. You may feel terrified of damaging your children in the same way that you yourself were harmed. Or you may worry that your children will become alcoholics. Perhaps you are afraid that they have inherited a genetic tendency for alcoholism or addictive behavior in general.

Your childhood experiences may make it difficult for you to be the kind of parent you want to be because you lacked good role models. As a child, you may have witnessed angry outbursts and violence instead of consistent, sensitive attention. Your family life may have been chaotic and unpredictable, and your parent's addiction may have caused financial problems. Perhaps you were forced to become responsible for yourself or for younger siblings at an early age. Because of various problems in your family of origin, you may be unsure about how or when to set limits, provide consistency and structure, or give your children responsibilities.

Remember that the difficulties you face as a parent are not your fault. Good parenting does not come naturally. What comes naturally is to treat your children the way you yourself were treated. If your alcoholic parent frequently yelled at you, then you will probably have a strong urge to yell at your own children when they irritate you, even if you are not an alcoholic.

Many cities have support groups for adult children of alcoholics. I highly recommend these groups if you grew up with an alcoholic or drug-addicted parent. It can be deeply healing to share experiences and feelings with other adults who suffered in the same way you did. You can offer each other emotional support as you work through your painful childhood. This kind of therapy will help you be a better parent overall, and you may gain perspective and insights that will help you raise your children to resist drugs and alcohol.

You may also find it useful to supplement a support group with information from parenting books or workshops to learn positive and effective parenting skills. You may have a pretty clear idea of how you do *not* want to raise your children but feel uncertain about what to do instead. The best way to judge the parenting advice you receive is to ask yourself the following question: "Is this how I would have wanted my parents to treat me?" If you can honestly answer yes to that question, then you have probably found wise advice. If you cannot answer yes, I recommend that you keep searching for an approach that feels right for you and your family.

Tip 6

Protect your child from physical and sexual abuse.

Physical and sexual abuse can lead to many problems later on, including violence, anxiety, depression, eating disorders, illnesses, and addictions. Teens who regularly use drugs are more likely to have been abused as children, either physically or sexually, than teens who do not use drugs.

It is vitally important to protect your child to the best of your ability. Don't leave your child with any person you cannot totally trust—even family members. If you have a "funny feeling" about Uncle Henry, trust that feeling. If your child suddenly resists being left with a baby sitter or in a daycare center after having been quite happy there, check carefully into the possible causes, and consider the possibility of physical or sexual abuse.

If your child has been abused, it is important to give him extra love and support, as well as professional therapy. Assure your child that the abuse was not his fault, no matter what was said or done. It's also important to confront the abuser, even if he is a member of your own family, and to take legal action. Otherwise, he will not get the help he needs and will continue to abuse children. Be sure to find support for yourself, especially if you have overwhelming feelings of anger or if the abuse triggers a memory of abuse from your own childhood.

Most abusive adults were abused themselves as children, and the cycle of abuse can pass from one generation to the next. However, not all abused children grow up to be abusive toward their own children; if you were physically or sexually abused as a child, take comfort from the fact that your painful past will not automatically turn you into an abusive parent. However, unless you find ways to heal from your past trauma, you may struggle to avoid harming your own child in similar ways. If you have strong urges to abuse your child (either physically or sexually), don't be afraid to ask for professional help and support. Find a therapist or join a support group of people who have experienced similar childhood trauma. You will probably find the experience to be beneficial and healing. There is nothing shameful about asking for the support you need to stop the cycle of abuse. On the contrary, it is an act of courage for yourself and your family.

Tip 7

Don't spank your child.

There is no research showing that spanking benefits children in any way, and many countries have made spanking illegal. Numerous research studies have shown that spanking is less effective than other methods of discipline and that it correlates with later violence, depression, and substance abuse, just like physical or sexual abuse. Corporal punishment, therefore, has no place in raising drug-free children.

Some people claim that spanking is okay because they were spanked as children and they turned out okay. This is the same faulty reasoning used by those who say it's okay to smoke because not all smokers get lung cancer. The fact is that there is a definite correlation between smoking and lung cancer, just as there is a correlation between spanking and a host of later problems. Furthermore, although people who were spanked as children might indeed function well as adults, at least outwardly, they may suffer from depression or violent rages without linking these problems to the early stress of corporal punishment.

There are several factors in the correlation between corporal punishment and later substance abuse:

- Corporal punishment can lead to anger and rebellion. Children often use drugs as a way to rebel against their parents.
- Corporal punishment shows disrespect for a child's body. Children who do not respect their bodies are more likely

to use drugs and to disregard their body's signals, making them vulnerable to overdosing.

- Corporal punishment can lead to low self-esteem. Children with low self-esteem are more likely to use drugs to feel accepted by their peers.
- Corporal punishment can cause chronic anxiety. Anxious children are more likely to use drugs.
- Corporal punishment prevents constructive communication. Parents and children who cannot communicate well about everyday conflicts will find it hard to talk about drugs.
- Corporal punishment can lead to lying and deception to avoid getting caught. Children who are in the habit of hiding things from their parents will continue doing so when they experiment with drugs.
- Corporal punishment can cause children to fear or hate their parents. Children who fear or hate their parents will want to leave home as soon as possible and are likely to reject their parents' values.
- Corporal punishment is emotionally and physically painful. Children exposed to frequent painful experiences are more likely to crave pleasurable experiences. Drugs provide pleasurable experiences.

This book includes numerous tips for setting appropriate limits without spanking children. I have also provided a list of recommended parenting books in Resources, at the back of the book.

Tip 8

Create a climate of emotional safety.

To grow up emotionally healthy and drug resistant, children need to feel physically and emotionally safe. You can create physical safety by meeting your children's physical needs (such as shelter, clothing, and food) and by protecting them from physical pain. Likewise, you can create emotional safety by meeting your children's emotional needs and protecting them from emotional pain. The following guidelines will help your children feel emotionally safe:

- Provide lots of physical closeness. When your children are little, hold them as much as they wish in your arms or on your lap. As they grow older, give them hugs and offer to massage their back or shoulders.
- Spend time with your children. Get down on the floor and play with them. When they are older, talk with them and express interest in their activities.
- Treat your children with respect. Treat your children at least as well as you would treat a close friend. Don't criticize or yell at them. Listen respectfully. Take their needs and feelings into account, and respect their privacy.
- Allow your children to express emotions. Expressing emotions freely can help children heal from painful experiences and feel emotionally safe, so don't ever shame, punish, or even distract your children from crying.
- Use a nonpunitive approach to discipline. Spanking can damage your children's sense of physical and emotional safety. (See the previous tip.) But nonviolent forms of

punishment (such as withholding privileges, creating artificial "consequences," or isolating your child) can also damage your child's sense of emotional safety. Many parents have the false assumption that the only alternative to authoritarian discipline is permissiveness. Later tips in this book will help you raise your children to be responsible, compassionate, self-disciplined, and drug free without using any kind of punishment.

- Don't sacrifice your own needs to the point of becoming resentful toward your children, as this also can damage their sense of emotional safety. Try to be aware of your own needs for rest, recreation, and adult companionship, and find ways to meet them without depriving your children of their needs.

This book provides various tips at different ages for implementing these suggestions and creating a climate of emotional safety. As you know, children are not always easy to live with. They are often noisy, messy, fussy, impulsive, curious, demanding, stubborn, forgetful, fearful, and self-centered. But they can also be wonderfully creative, compassionate, and cooperative. Try to accept your children as they are, and realize that they are growing and learning with your love and support.

Tip 9

Find healthy ways to cope with stress.

Your child will learn from you how to cope with stress. If your usual response is to take a drug when you are stressed, whether it's alcohol or a tranquilizer, your child will learn that consuming a chemical substance is an appropriate way to cope with stress. Be aware of nonchemical distractions or addictions as well, such as watching television, surfing the Internet, gambling, and overeating.

The way you cope with interpersonal conflicts with your partner will also have an impact on your child. Studies have found that children and teenagers whose parents have hostile conflict styles with each other have more problem behaviors than those whose parents solve their conflicts more peacefully. Interestingly, the *frequency* of disagreements does not matter as much as the way in which the parents resolve them.

Take the following self-test to become more aware of how you cope with stress. Check all the things you do when you are stressed.

_____ I become verbally or physically abusive.

_____ I withdraw.

_____ I put my own needs aside and take care of others.

_____ I drink alcohol, smoke, or use other drugs (legal or illegal).

_____ I bite my fingernails.

_____ I overeat or I forget to eat.

_____ I watch TV or go online.

_____ I go shopping.

_____ I cope well but eventually become ill.

_____ I make sure that I get enough exercise and rest.

_____ I address the sources of stress and try to minimize them.

_____ I find a supportive listener with whom I can talk and cry.

_____ I calm myself with breathing exercises, meditation, or yoga.

If you checked the last four items, then you are coping with stress in healthy ways. If you checked some of the other answers, you need to find better ways to cope with stress. Don't blame yourself. You probably lacked good role models when you were a child, and you were probably not encouraged to express painful emotions. By learning to cope with stress in healthier ways you will be a helpful role model for your children.

A word of caution: If you plan to withdraw from a psychoactive drug (either legal or illegal), be sure to do so under close medical supervision and with a supportive network of family and friends.

Tip 10

Look for the true sources of your anger at your children.

Your children will not feel emotionally safe if you have angry outbursts. Instead of blaming your children for your anger, look for the true sources. Possible external factors include a lack of financial or emotional support or insufficient help in caring for your children. Nuclear families, consisting only of parents and children, are a relatively recent phenomenon. Until the Industrial Revolution, there were usually numerous other family members who lived nearby. Nowadays, many families live hundreds of miles from their nearest relatives.

To counteract this lack of support, you will need to create your own "tribe," especially if you are a single parent or live far from other family members. Just as your children need to feel that they belong to a family and a community, you also need to belong to a larger community of caring individuals who can offer companionship, help, and emotional support in times of need.

There are also internal factors contributing to anger, and these are more complex. Parenting does not come easily to those of us who were ignored, spanked, abused, criticized, or yelled at. If you sometimes yell at your children without fully realizing where your anger comes from, look for the source of anger in your own childhood. Ask yourself whether your child or the situation reminds you of painful childhood events.

In my workshops for parents, I often do demonstrations on anger with individual volunteers. While searching for the root of their anger, these parents almost always discover a painful childhood memory that was triggered by their child's behavior.

These painful emotions from our own childhood become our emotional baggage, similar to a heavy backpack that we carry around with us. You may have the best intentions in the world but still find it hard to be loving and patient because of your emotional baggage.

To heal from your past, the first step is to admit that your own parents were not perfect. Try to see your parents realistically without idolizing them, no matter how much you love them. Then take the time to talk about your childhood memories with another adult, and don't be afraid to feel the painful emotions. Talk about the Sunday afternoon when your father slapped you because you woke him up from his nap, or the time your sister bit you and your mother unjustly accused you of starting the fight.

By finding support for the demanding work of parenting, and by expressing your feelings about your painful childhood experiences, you will find it easier to empathize with your own children and become more patient. You will also think more clearly during times of stress or conflict with your children. These benefits will allow you to establish a loving relationship with your children and create emotional safety for them, which is the basic foundation for drug resistance.

Tip 11

Live your values.

If you want your children to value the same things you do, it is important for you to model your values in the way you conduct your life. The example you set will be much more effective than a lecture. The following values are especially relevant in raising drug-free children.

- Altruism: Researchers have found that young adolescents whose parents emphasize altruism are less likely to associate with peers involved in deviant activities. To model altruism, you can help others in need or donate your money or time to worthy causes.
- Honesty: Your children's honesty will make it easier for you to discuss drug-related topics with them. You can model honesty by returning money if a salesperson gives you too much change. Don't flatter someone to their face and then criticize them behind their back. Be honest about your own imperfections, and don't be afraid to admit mistakes.
- Learning: If your children value learning, they will resist anything that might interfere with their education, such as taking drugs. Let your children observe you reading books for information and pleasure. Learn something new, such as how to create a Web page.
- Self-control: Modeling self-control will teach your children that immediate pleasures are not necessarily better than deferred ones. If you have a special treat for dessert, for example, resist the temptation to eat it up all at once.

Show your children how rewarding it is to save some for the following day.

- Respect for laws: This value has an obvious link to avoiding illegal drug use. One way to model it is to let your children see you obeying traffic regulations.
- Nonconformity: Modeling nonconformity teaches your children that it's okay to be different. Every family is unique, so rather than try to hide your family's uniqueness, be proud of it. When I was growing up, we did not own a television set because my father thought that watching TV was a waste of time. Although I felt different from my friends, I learned that they still liked me even though I didn't know who Elvis Presley was! This reassurance gave me the courage to know that I didn't have to conform to what other people did, and I was able to draw on that inner resource later on when someone offered me a marijuana joint. The courage to be different will send a powerful message to your children that it is okay to have values different from those of their friends. It will also help your children resist the pressure to conform, which is often an inherent part of advertisements for alcohol and tobacco.

Tip 12

Take care of your body.

If you take care of your body, your children will learn to do like-wise. A regular exercise program is essential for maintaining health. If your children know that you exercise regularly (with or without them), they will realize that exercise is a normal and regular part of life. It will become an integral aspect of their unconscious script for their life as adults.

During and after vigorous exercise your body produces en-dorphins. These chemicals are nature's tranquilizers and painkillers, and they are similar to the opiate drugs of mor-phine and heroin, so you can actually get "high" simply from exercising! If you are addicted to smoking, alcohol or drugs, you may find that a vigorous exercise program actually helps you overcome your dependency.

No time for exercise? Maybe you can walk or bike to work or jog for twenty minutes during your lunch break. You can also exercise with your children. When they are babies or toddlers, you can walk or jog with them in a stroller, or bicycle with them in a toddler bike seat. When your children are older, they can join you on walks, on bicycle rides, in the swimming pool, or on the basketball court.

Your children will learn safety precautions from you as well, so be sure to adopt those that you want to teach them. For ex-ample, wear a bicycle helmet, fasten your seat belt in the car, and wear a life jacket in a boat.

Another important aspect of your role modeling is to show your children that you pay close attention to what you put into your body. Take your children shopping with you, and let them watch while you carefully select healthy foods. Be sure to let them see you reading the list of ingredients on the labels of packaged or canned foods. Your children will learn to value the importance of what we eat if they see you checking for unnecessary food additives or substances that may trigger an allergic reaction. Likewise, if you or your children must take a prescription medication, let your children hear you ask the doctor or pharmacist about the possible side effects and potential interactions with other medications. Without saying a word to your children, they will learn by your example that it is very important to think carefully about what foods and medicines we consume. This understanding that our bodies are in need of attention and protection will serve your children well when they are exposed to dangerous drugs.

Chapter 2

Birth to Age 3

Tip 13

Strive for a drug-free pregnancy and birth.

This book would be incomplete without mentioning prenatal drug exposure because drug-free child rearing begins at conception.

During pregnancy it is important to avoid taking addictive drugs that could cross the placenta and enter directly into the fetus's blood. These substances can damage your baby's growing brain, cause malformations, and lead to premature birth and low birth weight. Some babies are born addicted to drugs, and that's not a good start in life. Additionally, prenatal exposure to tobacco, alcohol, and other drugs can lead to a tendency toward addictive behavior later in life, as well as hyperactive or inattentive behavior. If you are addicted to tobacco, alcohol, or illegal drugs, and if you are pregnant, now is the time to stop. But be sure to do so under close medical supervision.

Not all prescription medications are safe for your unborn baby, so be sure to let your doctor and pharmacist know that you are pregnant. Also check into the possible risks of nonprescription medications, including herbal remedies, before you consume any of them during pregnancy.

If your child is adopted, you may not know what drugs the mother consumed during pregnancy. If you know that your baby was exposed to drugs in the womb, don't hesitate to consult with specialists. Take advantage of any special programs offered in your community. Good parenting can help to reduce many of the possible negative effects of prenatal drug exposure. The human brain is still growing quickly during the first year after birth and is being shaped by experiences. If those experiences are positive and nurturing, your child's brain will develop as normally as it possibly can.

It is best to strive for an unmedicated birth. There is some evidence that exposure to opiate anesthetics (narcotics) during birth can predispose children toward opiate (heroin, morphine) addiction later in life. Classes in prepared childbirth can teach you breathing and relaxation techniques to carry you through labor without the need for medication. You will feel more relaxed and confident if you can choose your birth setting, attendants, and birthing position.

However, even with the best preparation, giving birth can be complicated and difficult. If you need pain relief during labor, this does not imply that you are weak. If you are offered a choice of medication, request a non-narcotic painkiller and an epidural, rather than a general, anesthetic.

Even if your child was exposed to drugs before (or during) birth, realize that he will not automatically become a drug addict! Prenatal drug exposure is only one of many factors predisposing children to drug use. It is entirely possible to grow up to be drug free in spite of prenatal drug exposure.

Tip 14

Breast-feed, but beware of drugs.

There are many advantages to breast-feeding. Although there is no conclusive evidence that breast-fed babies are more likely to resist drugs later on, it is possible that breast-feeding could have an indirect protective effect, for the following two reasons.

First, breast-feeding is the best way to start your baby on a lifelong path of putting healthy substances into her body. Human milk is the perfect food for infants, and it will give your infant all the nutrients she needs to grow a healthy body and brain during the first five to six months. Even after you introduce solid foods into your baby's diet, breast milk continues to be an important source of nourishment.

Second, breast-feeding guarantees physical closeness with your baby many times throughout the day and night. This closeness helps establish a strong bond between you and your baby. A close connection between parents and children is an important buffer for protecting children from drug abuse and other risky behaviors when they reach adolescence.

Although there are advantages to breast-feeding, there is no need to feel guilty if you are (or were) unable to breast-feed your baby. Your child can still feel loved and connected to you and can grow up to be healthy and drug free.

If you are a breast-feeding mother, it is very important to avoid drinking alcohol, smoking, or taking illegal drugs. Many of these substances go directly into your milk, and your baby may become addicted. Furthermore, these substances could damage your baby's brain, just as they can cause damage to a fetus before birth.

Be careful about prescription medication and over-the-counter medication as well, and let your doctor and pharmacist know that you are a breast-feeding mother before they write or fill a prescription for you.

If you need to take medication for medical reasons for only a few days, and if the medication is unsafe for your infant, you can feed your baby formula during that time and pump your milk and throw it away. The frequent pumping will be time-consuming, but it will help you maintain your milk supply and reduce the painful breast engorgement you would feel if you suddenly stopped nursing. Be sure to check with your doctor to find out the length of time the drug stays in your body. You may benefit from the support of a lactation consultant as well.

Tip 15

Never leave your baby to cry alone.

The term "cry it out" (also called "controlled crying") refers to the practice of leaving babies in their cribs without picking them up, and letting them cry themselves to sleep. A modified version of this approach is to go to the baby every few minutes to pat him on the back or reassure him verbally, without picking him up. The idea is to teach babies to fall asleep alone.

I do *not* recommend any kind of cry-it-out approach. Babies can feel terrified when nobody responds, and this abandonment can lead to feelings of powerlessness, lack of trust, low self-esteem, and chronic anxiety later in life. The cry-it-out approach undermines the very basis of secure attachment, which requires prompt responsiveness to infants.

Crying does not always indicate an immediate need. Instead, it may indicate a baby's need to release stress resulting from accumulated frustrations or frightening experiences. Some babies are easily overwhelmed by too much stimulation or changes in routine. Studies have found that babies who had a difficult birth cry more than those whose births went more smoothly. Protect your infant from stress, but realize that some stress is inevitable.

When your baby is still fussy after you have checked for all immediate needs and discomforts, I recommend the "crying-in-arms" approach rather than the "cry-it-out" approach. Pick your baby up and hold him while allowing him to cry in your arms. Eventually your baby will fall asleep in your arms or become calm and alert. This approach can be difficult to implement, so be sure to get plenty of support for yourself as well as time away from your baby so you can be relaxed while holding him through his crying spells.

Holding your baby when he cries is an excellent way to let him know that you will always be responsive to his needs and available to listen to his painful emotions and that you will love him no matter what he is feeling. If you continue to respond attentively as he grows older, he will bring his problems to you throughout childhood and adolescence, because he will trust in your ability to help or comfort him. It is wonderful when a teenager feels safe enough to cry in his mother's or father's arms. This closeness, confidence, and trust will help inoculate your child against drugs.

If you have used the cry-it-out approach in the past, there is no need to feel guilty. You did your best with the resources and information available to you at the time. Realize that it is never too late to rebuild the trust and establish a good listening relationship with your child.

A word of caution: Consult a doctor immediately if your baby cries a lot, if his crying suddenly increases or has an unusual sound, or if you suspect pain or illness.

Tip 16

Don't give your baby drugs to sleep.

For centuries, people have drugged fussy infants to make them stop crying and go to sleep. In the second century AD, the Greek physician Galen prescribed opium to calm fussy babies. In Europe, mothers made teething rags for babies by dipping pieces of cloth in alcoholic cider or filling small bags of linen with sugar and poppy seeds (the source of opium). Nursing mothers and wet nurses commonly smeared their nipples with lotions containing opium before breast-feeding their babies. The drugged babies slept quite soundly. Unfortunately, many of them became addicted to opium, while others died from overdose. An opium-based colic remedy for infants, called "Winslow's soothing syrup," was available in the United States without a prescription as recently as 1900.

It is no longer considered acceptable to give alcohol or opium to infants. However, other medications (such as antihistamines or anticholinergics) are sometimes used for fussy babies, even though organic causes account for less than 5 percent of infants with prolonged, unexplained crying spells. Although these drugs are not addictive, it is important to weigh the short-term benefits against the potential long-term consequences. Early exposure to these chemicals, many of which cause sleepiness, may predispose your child to seek relaxation later on through chemical substances. It is therefore wise to avoid medication to help your baby sleep unless the drug is needed for a medical reason.

If your baby has difficulty going to sleep or staying asleep, you deserve all the help you can find. If your baby is healthy but seems determined to cry after all of her immediate needs are met, you can allow her to release stress by implementing the "crying-in-arms" approach, which is described in the previous tip. Cradle your baby lovingly in your arms and allow her to cry freely as long as she needs to. A good cry in the safety and comfort of your arms can help your fussy baby relax and sleep well. I have been teaching this approach to parents for over twenty years, and the reports are highly encouraging. Many parents find that their baby soon begins to sleep better.

If your baby continues to awaken at night, remember that this problem will not last forever. Think of these years as an investment in your child's future. The more time you devote to her during the first few years, the fewer problems you will have later on. And don't hesitate to ask for help from family and friends so you can obtain the rest you need.

A word of caution: Consult a doctor immediately if your baby cries a lot, if his crying suddenly increases or has an unusual sound, or if you suspect pain or illness.

Tip 17

Respect your child's body.

If you respect your child's body, he will learn to value and take care of himself, and he will naturally resist anything that could harm his body later on, such as taking drugs. Here are some of the ways you can show respect for your child's body.

1. Hold your baby as much as possible. Babies thrive on physical contact, which helps them to feel loved and protected, so don't be afraid of "spoiling" your baby. Be loving and gentle during the care-taking routines of dressing, diapering, bathing, and feeding. Don't assume that your baby wants to be held by strangers. Follow your baby's cues.

2. Explain what you are going to do. You can say, for example, "Now I'm going to change your diaper, so I need to lie you down on your back." Then gently lay your baby down. When you bring your baby to a doctor, explain what the doctor will do, no matter how young your baby is. Say, for example, "Now the doctor is going to look into your ears."

3. Caress or massage your baby. Take a few minutes during the dressing and diapering routines to gently caress your baby's body with your fingers or with a soft piece of wool or fur. When he is a few months old, you can begin to give your baby massages by gently rubbing his back, limbs, and shoulders.

4. Never hit or spank your child. Corporal punishment shows disrespect for your child's body. Raising your children without violence may be difficult for you if your own

parents frequently hit or spanked you, and you may find yourself struggling with impatience or anger. Studies have shown that during the ages of birth to three years, there are two potent anger triggers for parents: prolonged crying in infants and refusal to cooperate in toddlers. (See Tips 15 and 20.)

If you struggle with occasional urges to hit your child, try the following suggestions: sit on your hands, yell into a pillow, hit a pillow, take some deep breaths and count to ten, share your frustration with your spouse, call a friend, have a good cry, or find someone to watch your child and get out of the house. Also, be sure you are getting enough help and support, as well as time away from your child. Don't isolate yourself. Try to meet other parents of young children. If you have frequent urges to harm your child, join a support group or get counseling. You deserve all the help you can get.

By respecting your child's body through gentle handling, you will teach him to respect himself and his body, an important step in inoculating him against drugs.

Tip 18

Respect your child's attachment needs.

A healthy attachment to parents during the first few years is important for children's emotional health and drug resistance. Adults who lacked an early secure relationship with their parents often suffer from depression, anxiety, and the inability to form healthy relationships. These painful feelings can cause a person to use alcohol or drugs. Experiments with adult monkeys, who were offered a choice of alcohol or water, showed that those who were deprived of early contact with their mothers drank more alcohol.

You can foster healthy attachment by frequently holding your baby, responding sensitively, and minimizing separations. Both parents can play an equally important role. In fact, infants can become attached to several people, and they benefit from more than one primary attachment figure.

A securely attached child is not necessarily independent. It is normal for your baby or toddler to protest when you leave her with a stranger, miss you when you are gone, want physical closeness when she is ill or frightened, and resist being left alone at bedtime. Babies and toddlers can play alone at times, but you cannot expect them to do so according to your schedule. There is nothing wrong with catering to these legitimate needs for closeness, comfort, and attention. Children eventually outgrow these early attachment needs and become independent, but they do so on their own timetable. If you try to force independence too soon, you may encounter resistance and conflict.

What about day care? Research has shown that placing an infant in day care for more than twenty hours a week during the first year can interfere with healthy attachment to her parents. If both parents must work outside the home during the first year, the best arrangement is for individual care from a close relative or a hired baby-sitter. If you must place your infant in group care, try to find a day care center near your work location so you can visit her during the day. A good-quality program can help to minimize the negative effects of group care, so look for a setting with warm, responsive caretakers and a high ratio of adults to infants.

Some countries allow lengthy maternity or paternity leave with full or partial pay. Unfortunately, this is not the case in the United States, so many parents must struggle to meet their financial needs while also meeting their babies' needs. You may not have much choice, especially if you are a single parent. There is no need to feel guilty if you must put your infant in day care, but do try to be as attentive as possible when you are with your baby. By nurturing a strong attachment with your child during the first few years, you will give her a solid feeling of security and high self-esteem, which will be the root of later drug resilience.

Tip 19

Allow your toddler to say "no."

The slogan "just say no" to drugs reflects the idea that resisting drugs starts with taking a simple but firm stand against peer pressure. This is an important factor in helping kids stay off drugs. However, learning to say "no" begins long before adolescence. Toddlers are very good at saying "no," and yet many parents think they should discourage or punish such behavior. When toddlers are punished for saying "no" to their parents, they may be ill equipped to say "no" later on to their peers. They may even associate taking a negative stand with fear of rejection.

Most toddlers go through a period of "negativism" between one and three years of age. This stage of development is healthy and normal. Toddlers want to assert themselves, and they practice saying "no" just as they practice other skills such as climbing stairs or feeding themselves. If your toddler experiences anger, rejection, or punishment, he will learn that saying "no" is risky business. This doesn't imply that you must bend your rules and let him do whatever he wants. But you can be firm without becoming angry or punishing him for saying "no," and you can allow him to express himself.

For situations that are not very important, allow your toddler to have the upper hand. For example, if you say, "You can wear your red shirt today," but your two-year-old says, "No!" it's okay to reply, "What color shirt would you like to wear?" and then let him choose another shirt.

For situations in which you cannot negotiate, such as putting your toddler in a car seat, first try some noncoercive methods for encouraging your child to cooperate. (See the next tip for suggestions.) If your child is still resistant, you may have to use force (but not violence) to put him into the car seat even though he protests strongly. Explain calmly why he needs to be buckled in, and avoid shaming him or becoming angry. Allow him to have his feelings, saying, "It's okay to be angry. I know you don't like sitting in your car seat." By being firm and matter-of-fact, but allowing your child to protest, you are letting him know that *it's okay for him to disagree with you*, even though, in that particular situation, you must override his wishes.

This stage may be difficult for you if you were punished for saying "no" to your own parents. You may feel impatient, angry, or even powerless with your strong and willful toddler. Try to remember that you are not the target and that your child is simply practicing a vital skill. Imagine your child as a teenager with the courage to say "no" to his peers who offer him alcohol or drugs. Think of these early years as training for that situation.

Tip 20

Elicit cooperation through nonauthoritarian methods.

Children between the ages of one and three years are notorious for refusing to comply with parental requests because they want to be autonomous. This normal stage of development can be extremely frustrating for parents.

You may be tempted to use punishments or rewards to make your child obey you. However, such an authoritarian approach can lead to rebellion later on, and drug use is often a way that teens rebel against their parents. If you begin with a nonauthoritarian approach to discipline when your child is little, you will establish a relationship of mutual respect, and your child will have no need to rebel during adolescence.

The key to getting your toddler to cooperate, without using either punishments or rewards, is to make the activity fun and give choices. Toddlers are much more willing to cooperate if the activity seems like a game and if they have some power to control the situation. Keep in mind, however, that toddlers can handle only a few limited choices, so don't overwhelm your child with too many. Also, avoid asking a question when there is no real choice, such as "Would you like to sit in your car seat?"

Examples of noncoercive methods to elicit cooperation in toddlers include the following:

- Brushing teeth: If your toddler refuses to let you brush her teeth, brush teddy bear's teeth first, let her choose between two different toothbrushes, or let her tell you when she is ready.

- Sitting in a car seat: If your toddler refuses to sit in her car seat, let her select a few toys to bring along, or sing a song while putting her in it.
- Putting toys away: Have an evening family cleanup ritual beginning with a special song. Make it fun. Pretend that the toys are mice scurrying home into their boxes.
- Diaper changing: Let your toddler choose to lie down or stand up during diaper changes. Many toddlers prefer to stand. Give her special toys to play with, or sing a song.
- Keeping your child safe near busy streets: Give your child a choice between riding in a stroller or holding your hand. Make it clear that there are no other options.

In addition to these suggestions, it is also important to give your toddler information about *why* you want her to do something. Explain your reasons, and don't underestimate your child's ability to understand. Instead of saying, "Don't throw the golf ball in the house," try saying, "That ball might break the window." You may be surprised at your toddler's willingness to comply when she has the necessary information. With these tips, you will build a good relationship with your toddler and avoid the pitfalls of authoritarian discipline.

Tip 21

Be patient with temper tantrums.

Many parents feel that children are misbehaving or being "manipulative" when they have temper tantrums. However, research has shown that crying and raging have beneficial effects on the body and mind and are a healthy way to release stress. I therefore recommend a tolerant and accepting attitude toward temper tantrums.

Teens and adults who abuse drugs often do so to manage and control painful emotions. Children therefore need to learn that it is safe for them to express sadness and anger.

Once a tantrum has started, it is *not* helpful to use punishment or time-out to get your child to stop screaming. This will only increase your child's frustration. Tell your child that you will stay with him until he feels better. Show him that *his anger cannot destroy the bond between you.* The tantrum will pass, and you will then find yourself with a child who is calm and cooperative.

This is not a permissive approach; accepting your child's emotions is *not* the same as allowing him to do whatever he wants. If a reasonable limit has triggered a tantrum, there is no need to "give in" by changing your mind. If you must hold your child firmly to prevent him from hitting his baby brother, you can keep holding him but accept his right to express his anger through crying and screaming. If you have already told your child that you will not buy ice cream at the store, you don't have to buy ice cream to placate him simply because he throws a tantrum. The important thing is to accept your child's emotions.

If your toddler has frequent temper tantrums, look for sources of stress and frustration. Did he have a hard day or a disappointment? Is there tension in the home? Has there been a recent change (such as a new baby)? Has something frightening happened? Toddlers need opportunities to do things themselves and make some of their own decisions, so give your child some autonomy. You can also minimize frustrations by adopting a nonpunitive approach to discipline. Some tantrums are inevitable. Research has shown that frequent tantrums often precede the acquisition of new skills such as walking or talking. Parents often observe a burst of language or motor development following a period of frequent tantrums.

A common occurrence is what I call the "broken cookie phenomenon." Your child may burst into a screaming rage about a minor event such as a broken cookie because it gives him an excuse to cry about an accumulation of minor upsets. Adults also have "broken cookie" days. Have you ever burst into angry tears after a stressful day simply because your partner was a little impatient with you? By accepting your child's need to vent frustrations, you will help him grow up free of painful, pent-up emotions, and this will decrease his need to keep feelings in check later on by using drugs.

Tip 22

Don't force your child to eat.

It is your job to make sure that your toddler eats wholesome foods, but *forcing* your child to eat is never a good idea. Babies are born with a natural tendency to know how much food their body needs, and they will spontaneously select a balanced diet for themselves if they are offered a variety of healthy food choices. You can therefore trust your child to become self-regulated.

If you force your child to eat more than she wants, you may inadvertently cause her to lose the ability to recognize her body's natural signals about appetite and fullness. This loss could lead to a habit of overeating, resulting in obesity. Overeating can, in turn, be a contributing factor to later drug use, as overweight teenagers sometimes begin smoking or use stimulants to curb their appetite in hopes that they will lose weight.

The tendency to disregard hunger signals can also contribute to drug use in another way. Children who have been forced to eat what their parents say is good for them may transfer that behavior to what others say is good for them (such as drugs) instead of trusting their own judgment. Then, having learned to disregard their body's signals, they may fail to notice symptoms in themselves of drug overdose.

Another problem with forcing your child to eat is that this creates conflicts between the two of you over food issues. These conflicts may damage your relationship with your child, which could set the stage for rebellion.

It is therefore important to trust your child's natural appetite and let her become a self-regulated eater. You can offer a small range of healthy choices at each meal, and let her choose what to eat. Keep in mind that it is normal for toddlers to have food "binges." For example, your toddler may crave fatty foods from time to time. These preferences usually reflect a genuine physiological need and are nothing to worry about.

There is no need to force or trick your baby to eat or even to comment on what she eats. You job is to offer wholesome foods. If you trust your baby's natural appetite, you will avoid conflicts over food, which are impossible to win anyway. You will also allow your child to pay attention to her body's signals and learn to respect her body's needs. Later on, this respect for the wisdom of her own body will be vitally important when someone offers her drugs.

A word of caution: If your child is not gaining weight normally, is overweight, or is suffering from other medical problems, it is important to obtain a medical evaluation.

Tip 23

Teach your child emotional literacy.

Most alcoholics and drug addicts are acutely aware of painful feelings but confused about their real needs. They use drugs to mask their painful feelings and to meet their *perceived* needs. It is therefore important for children to grow up knowing exactly what they need and how they feel and to have their needs and feelings accurately acknowledged and responded to.

You can help your baby learn to differentiate his various feelings and needs by paying close attention to his cues and trying to respond appropriately. Don't assume, for example, that every whimper implies hunger or a need to suck. Sometimes feelings of sadness, fear, or anger are harder to deal with than immediate needs such as hunger or coldness because often there is no specific need other than to be held and loved.

Sometimes your baby will need to cry in your arms to work through sadness, or your toddler will need to throw a temper tantrum to release pent-up frustrations. Stay with him and allow him to release his emotions until he feels better. Your child will learn that it's okay to have painful feelings and that they will eventually go away. Don't tell your child that he should feel differently, and don't try to stop him from expressing his feelings. In substance abuse recovery programs, former addicts must learn to accept their painful emotions without trying to blot them out with drugs.

The use of verbal labels for needs and feelings can take away some of the mystery and confusion and help your child feel understood. You can begin teaching your child emotional literacy from birth on, by reflecting back verbally what you think he needs or feels. For example, when your infant begins to cry several hours after a feeding, you can say, "Maybe you're hungry." When your baby seems bored, ask, "Are you bored?" and then find something for him to do. When a dog barks and frightens your toddler, you can say, "That dog frightened you." It's okay to use bigger words, too, such as excited, frustrated, disappointed, confused, curious, impatient, or jealous. Your child will understand these words long before he can use them himself.

By two years of age, you can expect your child to understand the words for basic needs and feelings and to communicate these accurately (either verbally or nonverbally, depending on his language skills).

Basic Needs

- Food (or beverage): I'm hungry (or thirsty).
- Rest/sleep: I'm tired.
- Physical contact: Hold me.
- Attention or stimulation: Play with me.

Basic Feelings

- Joy, pleasure: I'm happy.
- Sadness: I'm sad.
- Anger, frustration: I'm mad.
- Fear: I'm scared.
- Specific likes, dislikes, and preferences: I like Grandma. I don't like bananas.

Chapter 3

Ages 3 to 6

Tip 24

Play with your child.

Children who feel connected to their parents will not be desperate to belong to a peer group outside the family when they are older and will therefore choose their friends wisely. One of the best ways to maintain a good connection with your child is to spend time playing with her.

Even though you may feel that you spend a lot of time with your child, you may be surprised to discover how little *quality* time you actually spend with her. I recommend scheduling a regular, special playtime, preferably for 30 to 60 minutes each day or at least several times a week. If you have more than one child, try to arrange for individual time with each child, even if it's only once a week.

During this special time, let your child know that you will not answer the phone or tolerate any interruptions from other people in the family. You can even set a timer so your child will know that you will pay attention to her until the bell rings.

Making decisions is an important skill, so let your child decide how she wants to spend the time with you, and then do whatever she asks you to do. Try to honor your child's requests, whether it's building with blocks, joining her in make-believe scenes, or even playing in the mud. If you follow her lead, you will help her feel special and also increase her confidence in making choices. Try to resist the temptation to direct the play with your own ideas or turn it into a teaching situation. You will have many other opportunities to teach your child.

Don't forget the importance of reading to your child. Cuddling and sharing a book together can be a quality bonding experience, so try to read to your child every day.

I also recommend active games that promote laughter. If your child likes to play hide-and-go-seek, pretend that you cannot find her when she hides. If you play chasing games, run slowly enough so she can catch you. Pillow fights are especially popular with young children. Give your child a pillow and let her knock you down with it. If you pretend to be weak and fall dramatically onto the floor, she will probably laugh and want to play this game over and over again. Laughter is an important stress-release mechanism, so these games can be both relaxing and fun.

Special time and laughter games are wonderful ways to help your child feel loved and connected, learn to make decisions, and release tensions. All of these factors will contribute to your child's drug resistance.

Tip 25

Don't punish your child.

There is a myth that we must make children feel bad in order to change their behavior, and this fallacy is at the root of authoritarian discipline. It is true that painful consequences can produce children who are quiet and obedient, at least when they are young. However, punishment can have long-term negative results, which numerous research studies have revealed.

Corporal punishment (spanking or hitting) is especially damaging to your relationship with your child and to your child's self-esteem (see Tip 7). However, *all* punishment is damaging to children, including withdrawal of privileges, extra chores, and isolation. (See the next tip for the disadvantages of using time-out.) Studies have shown that punitive approaches to discipline can be at the root of adolescent problem behaviors, most likely due to the fact that children who are raised with punishment tend to rebel later on.

When trying to change your child's behavior without using punishment, the key is to look beneath the surface and to address the underlying cause. If you understand the reason for your child's behavior, it becomes much easier to change the behavior and meet everyone's needs without the use of punishment.

There are three underlying reasons for misbehavior:

1. The child has a legitimate need. Perhaps he is hungry, tired, or simply needs some attention.
2. The child lacks information. Children are not born knowing that windows can break, that teeth can get cavities, or that busy streets are dangerous.

3. The child is upset. He could be feeling frustrated, jealous, bored, frightened, or overstimulated. For example, a child's aggressive behavior can be caused by his parents' divorce. Resistance to bedtime can be caused by a fear of the dark.

There is a common misconception that a lack of punishment automatically leads to an overly permissive approach. However, it is entirely possible to set limits on your child's behavior without using punishment. I call this approach democratic discipline, and it is quite different from permissiveness. Having raised two well-adjusted and drug-free children without ever punishing them, I know it's possible. Like all parents, I made mistakes and learned through trial and error. This nonpunitive approach may not come easily if you lacked appropriate role models. It takes time and effort to learn how to be firm and loving while avoiding the use of punishment.

Some of the other tips in this book provide information for implementing democratic discipline. You will find additional support in Resources.

Tip 26

Don't isolate your child to control her behavior.

In a well-meaning effort to avoid hitting or yelling, the use of time-out has emerged as a popular approach and is recommended in many parenting books. Parents are advised to make their children sit on a chair or in another room while they ignore them. Although this method appears benign, it is an authoritarian and punitive approach with several problems.

Obviously, you don't send your child to time-out with the intention of making her feel unloved. Nevertheless, your child may *feel* unloved because she has no way of knowing that you still love her when you ignore her. Even if you say, "I love you," your actions speak much louder than your words, especially for children under six years of age. Your seeming rejection of her may cause her to feel anxious, insecure, and confused. Your child needs to feel loved *unconditionally,* not only when she behaves the way you want her to.

Additionally, if you isolate your child when she cries or has tantrums, she will learn that you are unable to tolerate strong emotions. Without a solid foundation of support for her emotional struggles, she will learn to hide her feelings from you. Later on, when she has problems as a teenager, she will assume that you are unable to help or listen. Having learned her lesson well, she will cut off communication with you by going to her room and closing the door.

Lastly, the use of time-out doesn't address the underlying cause of the behavior. If your child repeatedly pulls the cat's tail, she may simply be bored and may benefit from suggestions for something else to do. There is always a valid reason for children's behavior, and isolating your child will not solve the problem.

If you cannot determine the reason for your child's behavior, you can take a time-out together. Remove her from the situation *but stay with her.* You can discuss the problem behavior with her, listen to her feelings, and try to reach a mutually agreeable solution.

To become drug resilient, your child needs to feel a strong connection to you. You can establish this bond by showing unconditional love, meeting her needs, accepting her emotions, and avoiding authoritarian discipline. The use of time-out fails to accomplish any of these goals and therefore risks damaging your connection to your child. I'm not implying that the use of time-out will *cause* your child to use drugs later on. However, if you avoid isolating your child to control her behavior and follow the other tips in this book for nonauthoritarian discipline, you will strengthen your relationship with your child and therefore her drug resistance.

Tip 27

Don't use rewards or bribes.

In an effort to avoid the use of punishment, it is tempting to use bribes to motivate children to clean up their toys, get dressed quickly, or leave a playground when it is time to go home. However, the risk of using rewards for obedience is that they will teach your child to do whatever brings immediate gratification. The major appeal of drugs is that they produce an immediate reward in the form of intense pleasure. A basic psychological principle is that the sooner a reward follows a behavior, the more strongly the behavior will be reinforced. That's why the most addictive drugs are the ones that reach the brain the quickest.

Instead of being the agents of manipulation with promises of enticing rewards, parents should teach children how *not* to be manipulated by anybody or anything, including drug dealers. The use of rewards and bribes undermines this important message.

It is especially risky to use food as a reward to control your child's behavior because your child will learn that it is okay to consume something just to feel good (rather than to satisfy hunger). He may later continue to reward himself by consuming substances that make him feel good, such as a drug like marijuana. Special treats are fine, as long as you don't use these foods to control your child's behavior.

When you want your child to cooperate with your requests, the two basic questions to ask yourself are, "What do I want my child to do?" and "What do I want his *reason* to be for doing it?" For example, do you want your child to leave the playground only to obtain the cookie you promised? Or do you want him to cooperate because he respects your need to go home and prepare dinner? The more general question is: Do you want your child to consider the consequences of his behavior to *others*, or only to *himself*?

Instead of using rewards to motivate your child to cooperate, try some of the following suggestions:

- Give an advanced warning: "When the CD is done, it will be time to put your toys away."
- Provide a reason for your request: "We need to go home now so I can start cooking dinner."
- Make the activity enjoyable: "Let's take turns brushing each other's teeth."
- Offer a choice instead of issuing a command: "Would you like to get dressed before or after breakfast?"
- Negotiate: Reach an agreement on the number of times your child may go down the slide before leaving the playground.
- Do it together: "Let's clean up this room together."

Tip 28

Turn off the TV.

There are several reasons why it is better to minimize screen time for young children. One disadvantage of TV, videos, or DVDs is the exposure to images of people smoking or using drugs. Even children's cartoons sometimes show drug use. In the film *Alice in Wonderland,* Alice drinks a mysterious substance that makes her grow taller or shorter. This film also shows a giant caterpillar smoking a water pipe. Drug-induced sleep is a common theme in children's classic movies, including *Snow White* and *The Wizard of Oz.* For example, Snow White falls into a comatose sleep after eating a poisoned apple and is later revived by a kiss.

Although these films do portray the potential risks of consuming certain substances, they can also be a source of misinformation. Because there are no long-term negative consequences for the characters, a young child might think that it can be fun or exciting to consume different substances. If your child watches these films, use the opportunity to discuss the difference between poison, medicine, and food and to correct any misperceptions your child might have. Tell your child, for example, that a kiss is not an effective antidote for a poison.

The content of children's films is only part of the problem. A major disadvantage of watching too much television is that the act of viewing a video screen puts children into an unnatural state of passivity and may cause them to lose the ability to entertain themselves. This loss of resourcefulness could then lead to chronic feelings of boredom in the absence of outside stimulation or entertainment. When children are older, those who have watched a lot of television may be more tempted to combat boredom with drugs, which offer exciting new forms of stimulation. In surveys, pre-teen and teen drug users frequently state boredom as the primary reason for their drug use.

If you are tempted to use television or videos as a baby-sitter, find other ways to keep your child busy when you need some time for yourself. Listening to recorded music or stories can keep young children happily occupied and does not produce the same amount of passivity as watching a screen. You can also keep special toys in a closet and bring them out at times when your child needs something to do. Encourage your child to color with crayons or build with blocks.

By encouraging creative activities rather than passive television watching, you will help your child learn to be resourceful. This skill will be useful later on in preventing boredom and reducing the risk of your child searching for quick and easy entertainment through drugs. You will also avoid inadvertent exposure to drug use in television programming until your child is old enough to understand the dangers involved.

Tip 29

Don't pressure your child to read.

Most parents want their children to learn to read as early as possible so they will be ready for school. However, pressuring your child to read will not be helpful. Children learn at different rates, and some children need more time to mature. There is no correlation between when a child first learns to read and his intelligence. In fact, many intelligent people, including Einstein, were late readers.

Overly high expectations can make your child feel like a failure when he doesn't live up to your expectations. Furthermore, pressuring your child communicates to him that you do not trust in his own ability to learn when he is ready to do so. Children who feel overly pressured by their parents to succeed in school are at risk for using marijuana and alcohol, sometimes before the age of twelve. These children are also at risk for taking stimulants later on to stay alert and enhance their ability to concentrate. Increasingly large numbers of children are not satisfied with coffee, and so they use other stimulants, such as methamphetamine or Ritalin, as study aids.

It is therefore wise to be relaxed about your child's reading ability. Try to be supportive of your child and encourage his pre-reading skills without putting too much pressure on him. However, this attitude does not imply that you should sit back and do nothing. It is possible to *encourage* your child to learn without *pressuring* him. Instead of imposing a daily session of flash cards or drilling your child in phonics, it is better simply to spend time each day reading to your child. Reading to children is an important activity for parents to do because it culti-

vates higher-level thinking in an informal, affectionate environment. Also, it will enhance your bond with your child and help
him create pleasant associations with books.

If you expose your child to the wonderful world of books,
you will lay the groundwork for a love of reading and later academic success. Children who learn to enjoy books from infancy on will *want* to learn to read, and they will be able to do
so when their brains have matured sufficiently. Your role modeling is also important. Let your child see *you* reading for both
information and pleasure.

By establishing a relaxed, trusting environment in which
your child's academic skills can develop without pressure, you
will help him avoid taking drugs later on to succeed in school
or cope with the stress of overly high expectations.

Tip 30

Let your child make decisions.

The inability to make good decisions is a factor contributing to drug abuse. If you give your child opportunities to make decisions and learn from the natural consequences of bad ones, you will help her learn this valuable skill. Later on, when she needs to make important decisions about drugs and sex, she will handle the decision-making process with confidence. The following are suggestions for helping your three- to six-year-old child become a good decision maker.

Money

Give your child a small amount of money and let her decide how to spend it. Take her to a toy store or a children's bookstore and give her total freedom to decide what to buy (although you will need to explain which items are within her price range). Some children are impulsive by nature, and they select the first toy that looks attractive. Let your child buy the toy, even if you know that she will not play with it much after the first day. The chance to practice spending money will help your child learn the drawbacks of being too impulsive.

Clothing

Let your child decide what to wear, within reason. If the weather is cool, let her feel the outside temperature, and ask her what clothing she thinks she needs to stay warm. If she chooses not to wear a jacket, let her go outside without one, but bring her jacket along in case she gets cold. Don't mention the jacket or offer it to her until she complains of being cold.

The next time she goes out in cold weather, she will under-stand the importance of wearing a jacket before getting cold.

Other Decisions

There are many other times when you can let your child make decisions. For example, you can let her help decide who to in-vite to her birthday party, how to arrange her room, where to go on Saturday afternoon, and which toys to take on a trip. The possibilities are endless.

Avoid false choices between two limited possibilities, one of which is a punishment. For example, the choice between whining or going to time-out is a false one because you are es-sentially telling your child either to obey you or be punished. That's not much of a choice.

Remember that children learn to be good decision makers by making *real* decisions, not by being told what to do. By giv-ing your child opportunities to make decisions, she will learn about the consequences of bad choices, and she will become a confident and responsible decision maker.

Tip 31

Encourage healthy eating, but trust your child's food preferences.

Part of drug-resistance education is learning to put healthy substances into our bodies. In the previous chapter I mentioned that it is best not to force babies or toddlers to eat (see Tip 22). After infancy, most children will continue to choose a wholesome diet if their parents do not try to force them to eat, so you can trust your child's natural appetite as he grows older.

One risk of trying to control your child's food intake is that he may lose the ability to respond to internal cues of hunger and fullness. Another risk is that your child may later rebel against you by refusing to eat, eating junk food, or experimenting with drugs. Parental control can backfire in another way: Children's distaste for specific foods increases when they are forced to eat them, while their preference increases for foods that are restricted.

Remember that it is normal for children between the ages of three and six years to eat very little and to have strong likes and dislikes. Later on, when your child's growth rate increases, he will naturally eat a greater quantity and variety of food. With the following suggestions, you can encourage your child to eat healthy foods while respecting his body's natural wisdom.

- Take your child shopping and let him help select foods.
- Let your child see you reading food labels.
- Grow some vegetables and teach your child how to take care of them.

- Let your child help prepare food (by stirring ingredients or arranging a plate of raw vegetables).
- Serve food in attractive ways (for example, cut slices of cheese into animal shapes).
- Serve specialties from different ethnic groups.
- Give your child choices at each meal and let him decide what he wants to eat.
- Let your child feed himself. Don't put food into his mouth.
- Encourage your child (but do not force him) to take one bite of a new food.
- Serve foods separately on his plate, in small portions.
- Don't force your child to finish what is on his plate.
- Don't be rigid about restricting sweets.
- Never use food or sweets as a reward.
- Be a good role model. Let your child see *you* eating healthy foods.
- Eat meals together as a family and make meal times relaxed and pleasant.
- Model good table manners rather than criticize your child's manners.
- Don't force your child to stay at the table after he has finished eating.

A word of caution: Consult a doctor if your child is overweight or underweight, or if he has food allergies or other medical problems.

Tip 32

Allow your child to cry.

Most people who are addicted to drugs struggle with pent-up feelings of grief, fear, or anger and don't know how to cope with them other than to mask them with the drug. During withdrawal, the person often experiences these painful emotions, which are no longer being blocked. In successful recovery programs, alcoholics and drug addicts must learn to accept these emotions without numbing themselves with chemical substances. These programs create a supportive atmosphere for the participants to talk and cry without being judged.

Studies have demonstrated that people are in a more relaxed state after crying, and those who cry more have fewer stress-related illnesses. Many therapists encourage their clients to cry because they know how beneficial it is. It is therefore important to allow your child to cry. Try to be supportive of her need to cry when a toy breaks, when she scrapes her knee, or when it rains on her birthday party.

Some parents think that children who cry a lot are immature, spoiled, or manipulative, so they try to stop the crying by punishing or isolating their children. Others try to distract their unhappy children with food or a game, thinking it is their role to make children feel better. I do not recommend any of these responses to a crying child.

When your child cries, even when she seems to be "overreacting," the most helpful response is to accept her emotions and listen respectfully. You can say, "You are very sad right now. It's okay to cry. I'll stay with you until you feel better." The storm will pass, and she will feel better. Your child needs to learn that painful feelings have a beginning and an end and that they will eventually go away if she can express them freely. This is a valuable lesson that most drug addicts never learned as children.

If you were not allowed to cry as a child, you might feel a strong urge to stop your child from crying in the same way that you yourself were stopped. For example, if your father frequently threatened you by saying, "If you don't stop crying, I'll *give* you something to cry about," you might be tempted to use that same phrase when your child cries. Or you may tend to repeat your grandmother's gentle words of comfort ("Hush, hush, don't cry"), without realizing that you are stopping a vital healing mechanism in your child.

If you were stopped from crying with some of these phrases, try to resist the urge to respond to your child in a similar way. One of the greatest gifts you can give your children is to accept their full range of emotions. They will learn that painful feelings are nothing to be afraid of and that it is okay to express them. When they are older, they will fail to understand why people would want to numb painful feelings with mind-altering drugs.

Tip 33

Allow your child to express fear and anger.

In addition to allowing your child to cry, it is also important to let him express fear and anger. As with sadness, bottled-up fear and anger can lead to problems later on, including the tendency to control the painful feelings with drugs. Expressing feelings freely during childhood helps reduce the amount of emotional baggage that your child will have as he grows older.

Young children have many fears due to a growing awareness of mortality and a lack of information. Common fears are of the dark, animals, monsters, bathtubs, and toilets. These fears are nothing to be overly concerned about. However, the way in which you respond to them can either help or hinder your child's emotional development.

If you acknowledge your child's fears with patience and understanding, he will feel accepted. Give him information while recognizing that some fears simply have to be outgrown. Don't force your child to do something that obviously terrifies him, but don't go out of your way to protect him from something that is harmless. If he is afraid of a puppy, encourage him to approach the dog and pet it.

You may find it more challenging to accept your child's anger, especially when it is directed at you. But it is important for children to know that the emotional bond between the two of you is stronger than their anger. So if your child says, "I hate you," realize that this is probably only a momentary feeling of frustration, perhaps because of a necessary limit that you set. There is no need to reprimand your child, nor should you change your limit. Contrary to what many parents fear, the more you allow your child to express angry emotions with you, the less likely he will be to use hurtful words with others.

If your child throws a temper tantrum, allow him to rage and acknowledge his feelings. Loud crying and raging will not escalate into violent behavior later on. On the contrary, this healthy emotional release process will help your child become calm, gentle, and cooperative. (See Tip 21.) If your child has frequent tantrums, however, it is important to look for ways to reduce stress and frustration in his life.

If your child hits or bites, realize that these behaviors are *not* a healthy release of anger. You will need to step in and stop the violence, while explaining that you must keep everyone safe. Restrain your child firmly but lovingly in your arms, and allow the angry tears to flow. The goal is to stop the violence but not the crying. Holding your child to protect himself or others is quite different from the use of punishment. Don't spank or isolate your child, and remember that *children are the most in need of loving attention when they act the least deserving of it.*

Tip 34

Teach your child how the human body works.

Between the ages of three and six years, your child will be ready to learn some basic facts about human physiology. By teaching your child how the body works, you will help her learn how drugs can harm her body and how to protect her body. When she is older, this information and appreciation for the wisdom of her body will help her resist activities that could harm her body, such as taking drugs.

Children this age are particularly interested in learning where things come from and where they go, so a good way to begin is with a discussion of digestion. Teach your child that the food we eat goes to our stomachs where it is broken down into tiny pieces. Then it goes to the intestines where useful substances are pulled out to enter the blood. The leftover waste products travel through the intestines and become fecal matter. (You can use your family's term for this.) Be sure to comment on the body's natural wisdom to know how to get rid of waste products.

This can lead to information about the blood and the heart. Tell your child that the blood carries nutrients to all the parts of our bodies, up to our brain and down to our very toes. The heart pumps the blood automatically, without our need to think about it. Tell your child that everything she consumes, whether it's food, medicine, or poison, is carried by her blood to every part of her body.

Next, you can explain that we need oxygen to live, and it is therefore important to breathe pure air with plenty of oxygen. When we inhale air with fumes in it, these can be toxic to us and can also prevent us from getting enough oxygen. This is important information that will help your child learn the dangers of smoking or using inhalants. Explain that whatever we breathe ends up in our blood.

Finally, give your child some basic information about the brain. Tell her that her brain controls all of her thoughts, movements, memories, and feelings and that it is very important to protect her brain. You can further reinforce this idea by insisting that your child wear a helmet when she rides a scooter or bicycle. Tell your child that small amounts of some substances can have a direct effect on the brain and can make us feel and act differently. Give examples of substances your child is familiar with, such as mild pain relievers.

If you wish to explain the concept of addiction, you can say that people sometimes take dangerous drugs or do other bad things that feel good, but then they can't stop doing those things. Use the examples of watching too much TV or eating too much chocolate to illustrate behaviors that are hard to stop, even though they are not good for us.

Tip 35

Teach your child the difference between poison,
medicine, and food.

It is important for children to learn the differences between
poison, medicine, and food. You can begin to teach your child
about these differences when he is three years old, or even earlier, by making use of times when the topic arises naturally
during everyday life.

Prescription drug abuse is common in adolescents. You can
help prevent it in your child by teaching him early on that
these substances can be dangerous. If your child must take
medicine, explain how it will help him, and give him the prescribed doses while emphasizing that it would be dangerous to
take more than the doctor prescribed. Tell your child that medicine is very strong and very special and that we take it only if
a doctor has told us to do so. It can be harmful if we take too
much of it or if we take it for some other ailment without consulting a doctor.

Be sure also to teach your child that combining different
medicines can be dangerous and that doctors need to know
what other medicines we are taking. For example, if your
child's doctor prescribes an antibiotic for an ear infection, be
sure your child hears you asking the doctor whether it is safe
for your child to also take a pain reliever. Medicine for children
is often fruit-flavored, just like candy. Teach your child that
medicine is different from candy or food, even if it tastes like
cherries or bananas. Keep all medicine locked up and out of
reach of young children.

You should also teach your child about poisons in your home, and keep them out of reach. It is especially important to give information about products with toxic fumes because children who use inhalants sometimes begin to do so before the age of twelve. Many household products can be inhaled for a cheap and short high. Don't wait until your child is older. Early childhood is the time to teach your child that these substances are dangerous. Unfortunately, most children and adolescents who use inhalants have no idea that the fumes can be deadly. They don't even think of inhaling ("huffing") as using drugs because they are not swallowing or injecting anything into their bodies. Popular inhalants are shoe polish, paint thinner, gasoline, lighter fluid, nail polish remover, spray paint, glue, certain felt-tipped markers, hair spray, and nitrous oxide. Some children first sniff these substances through chance encounters and then continue doing so because they think it's fun. If you keep any of these products in your home, use them outdoors or near an open window, and explain to your child that it is very dangerous to breathe the fumes.

Chapter 4

Ages 6 to 12

Tip 36

Listen nonjudgmentally to your child's problems.

Listening to your child is one of the most important ways to stay connected and make her feel loved, accepted, and understood. If your child is upset because of a mistake in a soccer game or because she was not invited to a birthday party, encourage her to express her feelings.

Sometimes it's helpful to reflect back (mirror) your child's feelings by saying, for example, "You seem really upset and disappointed about that soccer game." Other helpful comments are, "How did that make you feel?" or simply, "Tell me more. What happened next?" Sometimes you don't have to say anything at all, but just listen attentively and compassionately.

Most of the time, children do not want their parents to solve their problems for them. Although you will naturally want to share your wisdom, resist the urge to give advice. Your child needs the freedom to find her own solutions, and she may resent your advice if she has not specifically asked for it.

Another common mistake is to judge or blame children for their problems. Think about how you would feel if someone said to you, "If you had practiced the piano every day, you wouldn't have made all those mistakes in that recital." Even though you may think that your child's problem is caused by her own mistakes, it is *never* helpful to point this out to her, as she probably already knows this.

Be careful, too, not to deny your child's feelings in a well-meaning effort to cheer her up. Your child will not feel well listened to when you say, "Don't worry, I'm sure you'll do better next time." She needs you to acknowledge how bad she feels. Only then will she be able to move beyond the upset feelings. Children often feel so sad or frustrated that they cry. When a child of any age cries, the most helpful response is to follow the guidelines of good listening. Avoid giving advice, blaming your child, or trying to cheer her up. *Don't ever tell your child to stop crying,* even though you may feel that she is overreacting. People of all ages can benefit from a good cry, so don't imply that she is weak or childish. Your child needs your loving attention so she can release her painful feelings. After a good cry, she may surprise you by becoming spontaneously cheerful, perhaps even finding a creative solution to her problem.

One of the major causes of substance abuse in adolescents is the desire to keep painful emotions under control. Children who are free to express their emotions will have less of a need to resort to drugs later on. Therefore, anything you can do to help your child express painful emotions through talking or crying will strengthen her drug resilience.

Tip 37

Volunteer at your child's school.

Staying connected to your child can become more difficult as he grows older and as school, friends, sports, clubs, and other activities take up more of his time. It is normal and healthy for your child to enjoy spending increasingly more time with friends outside the family.

One way to stay connected is to volunteer at your child's school. Your child's teacher may welcome your offer to volunteer in the classroom on a weekly basis. If not, perhaps you can participate occasionally if you have special knowledge or a skill to share with your child's class. For example, when my daughter was ten years old, I arranged with her teacher to come to the school and talk to the children about writing books.

If the school does not welcome your participation in the classroom, you can offer to lead a fund-raising project, help with a field trip, volunteer in the school library, or assist with an end-of-the-year performance or party. If you are employed in a setting that would be of educational value for the children to visit, you can suggest a field trip to your place of work.

If the school has a parent/teacher association, join it. It is also important to attend the parent information meetings or social events that the school organizes. Be sure to attend school plays or concerts that your child is in, even if it means rearranging your work schedule. Try to meet with your child's teacher at least once during the year (preferably during the first three months of the school year), even if your child is not experiencing any problems.

One advantage of becoming involved with your child's school is that the information you gain about the school, as well as the friendly rapport you develop with the school staff, will be useful if your child should experience problems with his teachers, schoolwork, or friends. If your child later experiences school-related stress, you will be in a good position to help him. Tell your child that his teachers have the well-being of children at heart and that problems can usually be worked out through open and regular communication. Because school stress can be a contributing factor to substance abuse, this positive relationship with your child's school will help to reduce the risk of your child taking drugs to cope with school stress.

Another advantage of becoming involved is that you will let your child know that you are interested in his life and want to stay connected as he grows older. You will also convey the important message that education is important. A friendly connection with your child's teachers will show your child that you consider educators to be kind and important people who are worth getting to know. Children who feel connected to their families and schools and who value learning and education are less likely to experiment with drugs.

Tip 38

Encourage, but don't pressure, your child to be academically successful.

A common challenge parents face is to encourage children to be academically successful without putting too much pressure on them. Excessive pressure can lead to stress and to fear of failing to meet your high expectations. Overly high achievement pressure by parents is a risk factor for substance abuse in children. Children who feel pressured by their parents to get good grades sometimes begin using drugs as early as eleven to thirteen years of age. They find that alcohol, tobacco, or marijuana helps them relax and escape from the pressure to succeed, while stimulants such as Ritalin increase their alertness for studying or taking exams.

If your child's school uses a grading system, try to adopt a casual attitude. When your child brings home a good report card, you can simply say that you are pleased that she is learning in school. If your child has a low grade for a specific subject, you can say, "How do you feel about math (or reading)?" Your child may indicate that she dislikes her teacher, the instructional methods, or the reading material. You can also do your own independent assessment of your child's learning. If your child has earned a bad grade in reading, but you have observed at home that she is progressing in her ability to read, there is no need to worry. School assessments are not always a valid indication of learning.

If your child seems to be struggling in school, meet with your child's teacher to discuss the problem and hear the teacher's point of view. Perhaps your child would benefit from some extra tutoring or a special educational program. Slow learners are not necessarily less intelligent than other children, nor are they lazy. Sometimes they are maturing more slowly or have emotional problems. Perhaps your child finds it difficult to concentrate in school because of family stress. Or maybe the teaching methods do not match your child's learning style (see the next tip).

Remember to focus on *learning* rather than on *grades,* and avoid making your child feel bad if she earns a bad grade. Let your child know that mistakes on tests are an important part of the learning process. It is much better to offer encouragement and help rather than external control in the form of rewards or punishment. By not pressuring your child to be academically successful, you will help her to succeed in school while feeling good about herself. Your relaxed attitude will make her less likely to turn to drugs to cope with school stress or enhance her academic performance.

Tip 39

Be aware of your child's learning style.

Psychologists have distinguished seven different forms of intelligence, which give rise to different learning styles in children: 1) mathematical, 2) verbal, 3) visual, 4) kinesthetic (tactile and motor skills), 5) musical, 6) interpersonal (social intelligence), and 7) intrapersonal (self-awareness). Some identify an eighth one: naturalistic (sensitivity to nature). Some children are equally gifted in all of these areas, while others are more gifted in one or two. There are three reasons why it is important to be aware of your child's learning style: to help him succeed in school, to find effective approaches to discipline, and to know how best to communicate important information, such as facts about drugs.

Good teacher training programs emphasize teaching methods that address different learning styles. Even with excellent teachers, however, your child may have a hard time with the traditional academic subjects of reading and math if he is more gifted in some of the other forms of intelligence. You can let him know that there is nothing wrong with him, and you can help him learn school subjects through methods that make use of his unique learning style.

For example, if your child has strong kinesthetic intelligence (tactile and motor skills), you can help him learn the letters of the alphabet by cutting out sandpaper letters and letting him touch them. Explain addition and subtraction by asking him to jump forward or backward a specific numbers of times. By understanding your child's unique intelligence and learning style, you will help him become a successful learner, enhance his self-esteem, and reduce the risk of him turning to drugs later on to cope with school stress.

You can also adapt your discipline approach to your child's learning style. A highly verbal child will respond well to a written list of rules and to verbal problem-solving, while a highly visual child will benefit from visual reminders to do chores or brush teeth. Both you and your child will be less frustrated if you remember to take your child's learning style into account, and your child will be less likely to rebel.

An understanding of your child's learning style will also be useful to you when you begin to give him important information about drugs. If your child has strong mathematical intelligence, and you wish to explain the health dangers of smoking, tell him the percentage of people who get lung cancer from smoking. If your child has good interpersonal intelligence (social skills), he will probably be more impressed by stories of real people who have struggled with a smoking addiction. A child with strong visual intelligence may learn most effectively by seeing an image of a smoker's lungs.

Tip 40

Avoid stimulant medications.

The diagnosis of attention deficit hyperactivity disorder (ADHD) has increased significantly in the United States for children who are hyperactive, impulsive, or inattentive. Doctors often prescribe stimulants, such as methylphenidate (Ritalin), to control these children's behavior. However, not all psychiatrists agree that ADHD is a distinctive medical syndrome. In the majority of cases, there is no evidence that these behaviors are caused by any malfunction or chemical imbalance in the child's brain. Furthermore, there are numerous other possible reasons why children might have trouble sitting still, paying attention, or following instructions in school.

Prescription stimulants can make children more manageable by helping them focus on rote tasks. However, the disadvantages far outweigh the benefits. A child who is taking stimulant medication is, by definition, *not a drug-free child.* The percentage of children medicated with stimulants is much greater in the United States than in any other country, and some countries have even banned these medications.

The following is a list of evidence-based reasons to avoid giving stimulants to your child.

- They have potentially dangerous side effects, including an increase in blood pressure, suppression of growth, and insomnia.
- They diminish spontaneity, creativity, and problem-solving skills.

- The safety and efficacy of long-term use have not been established.
- They are addictive, with neurological effects similar to those of street drugs (amphetamine, methamphetamine, and cocaine).
- They are frequently abused by children and adolescents.
- Their use teaches children that it's okay to take drugs to control their behavior and mood.
- Withdrawal can result in a return of symptoms, as well as additional symptoms.
- They mask underlying problems and prevent parents, teachers, and doctors from finding alternative explanations and solutions.

I knew a bright six-year-old girl who couldn't sit still in school and whose teacher and doctor thought she should be given medication (Ritalin). Instead, her parents switched her to a school that allowed more movement, creativity, and hands-on learning. She directed numerous plays, which the children wrote and produced themselves, and she also flourished in a children's performing dance group. She has now grown into a confident and delightful young woman. What a shame it would have been to subdue that child's creativity and vitality with drugs!

Not all behavior problems are solved that easily. If your child has trouble adapting to a school environment, she would benefit from a diagnostic team including you, the teachers, a psychologist, and a pediatrician. Parenting is a difficult job, and you deserve all the information, help, and support you can find. But try not to settle for a deceptively easy solution in which the only real winners are the pharmaceutical companies. (See the next tip for alternatives to stimulant medication.)

A word of caution: If you wish to withdraw your child from stimulant medication, be sure to do so under close medical supervision.

Tip 41

Address the underlying causes of hyperactive or
inattentive behavior.

If your child is diagnosed with ADHD (hyperactive, impulsive,
or inattentive behavior), look for the underlying causes. Most
of the research on ADHD has focused on searching for elusive
biological causes and for drug-based treatments. There is very
little funding for research into other possible causes or treatments for children who are hyperactive or inattentive. Because
of this fact, practitioners are not trained to investigate the
sources of stress in a child's life or past sources of emotional
trauma, both of which can cause agitation and distractibility in
children.

Possible causes for hyperactive, inattentive, or impulsive behavior include the following:

- *Physical:* brain injury (from an illness, accident, or prenatal drug exposure), brain tumor, hormonal or nutritional
  deficiencies, toxins, medications, food allergies, ill health,
  pain, hunger, fatigue, vision or hearing problems, physical
  disabilities.
- *Psychological:* unhealed emotional trauma (for example,
  past abuse, neglect, hospitalization, separation from parents, death of a parent, parental divorce, natural disaster,
  terrorism), pent-up emotions (if the child is not allowed
  to cry or express anger).
- *Environmental:* unmet needs (for attention, affection, respect, stability, stimulation, or play), family or school

stress, inappropriate discipline or teaching methods, teasing or bullying, too much TV, sudden life change (for example, birth of a sibling, move to a new home), parental alcoholism or depression, media exposure to violence, real threats of violence (from parents, neighborhood gangs, war, or terrorism).

It is important to note that *none* of these causes justifies the use of stimulants.

There are several things you can do if your child is hyperactive, inattentive, or impulsive.

- Take your child to a doctor to rule out legitimate physical causes (such as those listed above).
- Minimize sources of stress in your child's life.
- Offer your child a well-balanced diet.
- Find a school that offers self-directed learning through movement, choices, and hands-on activities. If necessary, consider homeschooling.
- Minimize "screen time" (TV, DVDs, computer).
- Give your child plenty of unstructured time with opportunities to run, jump, dance, climb, build, and play with sand and water.
- Play with your child on a daily basis. Be nondirective but responsive. Laugh together.
- Avoid the use of punishments and rewards, which can cause resentment and frustration in children. Look for underlying reasons for behavior, and strive for mutual conflict resolution.

- Don't stop your child from crying or raging. Your child will be calmer, more cooperative, and more attentive after a good cry or tantrum (with your loving attention).

By implementing these suggestions and avoiding the use of stimulant medication, you can keep your child truly drug free. In over twenty years of my consulting experience with parents, I have not encountered a single child whose behavior failed to improve after the parents implemented the above suggestions.

Tip 42

Find after-school activities for your child.

The hours after school are often times when children first experiment with drugs, especially if they are unsupervised. You can prevent this from happening by making sure that your child has interesting activities to do after school.

Most cities offer a variety of after-school programs and classes for children. Find the ones that best suit your child's interests, whether it's a sport group, a chess club, a scout troop, a dance class, music instruction, or a volunteer activity such as walking the dogs at an animal shelter. The advantage of these activities is that they will give your child something constructive to do after school. They will also help your child meet other children with similar interests and gain self-confidence by developing skills and talents.

You can also organize interesting after-school activities in your own home. When your child comes home after school, it is important for you to be there. Children should not be left alone until they are at least twelve years old. They need the companionship and supervision of an older person who can listen, provide a healthy snack, and help with homework if necessary. Children who must fend for themselves after school sometimes feel stressed and lonely, and they are at risk for joining gangs and getting involved in drugs. So try to arrange your work schedule to be available for your child after school. If you cannot be home, arrange for someone else to be there or make other plans for your child (such as after-school day care or going home with a friend whose mother or father is home).

When your child arrives home, begin by listening to her. Encourage her to tell you about school and show you the papers or projects she has brought home. If something upsetting happened at school, listen compassionately to your child without judgment. Then suggest something fun for you to do together, such as a craft or cooking project. Even after she knows how to read, you can continue to read out loud to her. Play games, take a walk, play tennis, or go to a museum together. Offer to help her with her homework.

If you have more than one child, it is fun to do these activities together as a family. However, try to make an effort to spend some individual time with each child after school or in the evening, even if you can arrange only fifteen minutes per child.

By making sure that your child's after-school hours are filled with supervised, interesting, and wholesome activities, you will reduce the likelihood that she will seek entertainment through drugs.

Tip 43

Teach your child to cope with boredom.

In the previous tip I mentioned the importance of after-school activities for your child. Be careful, however, not to overschedule your child's life. Children also need downtime in which they are free to do whatever they please. Too much structure can cause your child to lose his inner resources and may lead to boredom at times when no activities are planned. Boredom is a contributing factor to drug use by teenagers, and there is no doubt that drugs provide entertainment, excitement, and novelty.

Children who watch too much television easily become bored when it's turned off because it provides passive entertainment and prevents them from developing their inner resources. Try to reach a mutual agreement with your child about television viewing, and encourage him to play, read, listen to music, and engage in creative activities.

Another factor that prevents children from developing their own inner resources is a very structured classroom that does not encourage free choice or self-directed learning. Most teachers aim to develop children's inner resources and creativity, but this goal is sometimes hard to accomplish in a traditional school setting.

For the first few years of elementary school, my children attended a public alternative school in which they had three hours of free choice time every morning. During the summer holidays, they were full of ideas for creative activities and never complained of boredom. At ten years of age they switched to a more traditional school with excellent teachers who offered challenging, enjoyable, and creative learning experiences. However, there was very little *choice* of activities, and the children were expected to do what they were told. Interestingly, my children complained of boredom during the summer holidays, claiming that they couldn't think of anything to do because they had become dependent on their teachers to direct them. Sometimes they needed several weeks to fully regain their ability to be self-directed. If your child attends a traditional, structured classroom, be sure to provide plenty of opportunities for free play after school, on the weekends, and during school holidays.

When your child complains of boredom, resist the urge to provide suggestions for activities. Instead, try the following exercise. Ask him if he would be willing to do nothing for at least ten minutes and fully experience boredom. Children who are used to being passively entertained or having their activities directed by others sometimes feel empty, confused, or even anxious when nobody tells them what to do, so let your child know what to expect. After ten minutes, ask him to share his thoughts and feelings with you. After this exercise, your child may find that the feeling of boredom has disappeared, and he may surprise you (and himself) by thinking of something to do.

By helping your child develop his own inner resources, you will lower his risk of experimenting with drugs to combat boredom.

Tip 44

Help your child find a peer group.

Between the ages of six and twelve years, children begin to look for peer groups outside of their immediate families. They need to feel that they belong to a wider community, which is why clubs are so popular at this age. Without some direction from you, however, your child might get involved in a group that could have a bad influence on your child. Children as young as eleven or twelve years are strongly influenced by the drinking behavior of their peers (although this influence is only one of many factors leading to alcohol consumption). If you take steps to direct your child toward the right kinds of peer groups from the start, your child will form friendships with other children in those groups. She will have a sense of belonging and will avoid peer groups that use drugs or alcohol.

If your child is naturally outgoing, she will probably have no problem finding friends. If she is shy, she may need more help. In either case, there are several steps you can take to steer your child in the right direction and help her find a good peer group.

One thing you can do is arrange informal get-togethers (such as song nights or picnics) with other families who share your values and child-rearing philosophy. Begin with your own extended family. If your child has cousins nearby, you can plan activities with them. The children don't have to be all the same age for friendships to form. You can also look for a peer group for your child among your neighbors, your religious community, or your child's classmates. Don't forget to help your child maintain previous relationships from nursery schools or day care centers to provide continuity in friendships. If you move to a new neighborhood, it will be especially important to help your child form new friendships as quickly as possible.

You can further encourage your child's social life by helping her become involved in activities with other children who share the same interests. In addition to structured after-school activities such as sports, scouts, or music, consider helping your child engage informally in activities with other children. Is your son interested in dinosaurs? Help him form a dinosaur club and suggest activities for the club to do, such as visiting a local museum or hosting a dinosaur party. Is your daughter fascinated by magic tricks? Suggest that she invite some friends over to prepare a magic show for younger children.

By helping your children pursue their interests with other children, you will be steering them toward wholesome friendships and meaningful activities.

Tip 45

Get to know your child's friends and their parents.

There are several advantages in getting to know your child's friends and their parents. One is that you will know the kinds of people that are influencing your child. Also, by getting to know the parents, you can verify your child's statements when he says, "All my friends get to do it," whether it's staying out late or riding a bicycle without a helmet. You may discover that these statements are exaggerated, and you can inform your child that most of his friends are *not* allowed to do those things. This information may help him to accept your safety rules.

Another advantage of knowing other parents is that you can help supervise each other's children and look out for their safety. When your child reaches an age at which some children begin to experiment with drugs, you can ask the other parents if they are aware of any drug use among your child's group of friends. Connecting with the families of your child's friends will help to form a safety net for your child.

The longer you live in the same city, and the smaller the city is, the more likely you will be to know the parents of your child's friends. We were fortunate to live in the same city during the entire time my children were growing up. When they were in high school, I knew many of their friends' parents, some from toddler play groups or previous schools they had attended, others from our neighborhood, and others from my own adult activities. If you have recently moved to a different city, you will need to make extra efforts to get to know the parents of your child's friends. There are lots of ways to meet your child's friends and their parents, including the following:

- Encourage your child to invite a friend to your home to play.
- Invite your child's friends and their parents to a meal in your home.
- Invite your child's friends and their parents to attend a special event with your family (for example, a circus).
- Volunteer at your child's school (help with field trips, fund-raising, etc.).
- Become a scout leader or a children's sports coach.
- Arrange to share driving with other parents for after-school activities such as sports or music.
- Attend family events at your child's school.
- If your child's school has a parent/teacher association, join it.
- Join a parenting class.
- Talk to your neighbors.
- Get involved in a social activity for families or adults in your neighborhood.
- Join a religious community in your neighborhood.
- Get involved in a neighborhood volunteer project.

Tip 46

Establish family traditions.

Family traditions and rituals help children feel connected to their family and culture. They provide unity, structure, and stability, and they mark passages or holidays in meaningful ways. Establish the ones that are the most meaningful and enjoyable for your family.

In adopting traditions based on your faith or cultural heritage, aim to develop your own family's unique way of celebrating, perhaps with special foods, songs, or decorations passed down from your own grandparents. These customs will provide your children with a deep connection to their roots. Try to blend traditions from both sides of your family, so your children will feel equally connected to both parents' families. This is especially important if the two parents come from different religious, racial, or cultural backgrounds.

You can also invent new traditions or rituals. Examples of new family rituals might be taking a family hike every year on the first day of spring or holding a family game night on Sunday evenings. One of the birthday traditions in our family is that each family member states, in turn, what he or she especially likes about the person whose birthday it is. At the end, the birthday person appreciates himself. If you invite your children to make suggestions for rituals, they will feel empowered when the whole family participates.

It is important to maintain rituals and traditions during times of stress or change. If your family moves to a new location, continue to honor your traditions even though you might not have finished unpacking all of your boxes! If there is an illness, death, divorce, or financial crisis in the family, try to maintain the traditions even though nobody feels like celebrating. Your child needs to know that life will go on as normally as possible in spite of the family's hardships. And don't assume that your children are ever too old for family traditions.

Holidays and other traditions can be stressful for your family if they involve too much work or if you or others have unrealistically high expectations. If you become stressed, overworked, or resentful during family celebrations, your child will have painful memories instead of pleasant ones. My advice is to keep these traditions simple, encourage everyone to help, and don't expect perfection.

By establishing family traditions, you will help your child feel connected and secure, and thereby increase her resilience to drugs.

Tip 47

Hold family meetings.

Interviews with teenagers have revealed that they often use drugs to rebel against their parents' authoritarian control, and numerous studies have shown that punitive discipline can lead to delinquent behavior. If you begin holding family meetings when your children are young, you will have a forum in place for establishing rules and solving conflicts in a nonauthoritarian, democratic way.

The effectiveness of family meetings is based on the well-established psychological principle that children are more likely to follow rules that they themselves have helped create through joint decision making rather than rules that have been set unilaterally in an authoritarian way. In a family meeting, everybody can bring up a problem, participate in finding a solution and making rules.

In our family, we had a regular weekly meeting time and a written agenda. We taped a blank sheet of paper to the refrigerator door during the week, and family members wrote down the items they wanted to discuss. This list became the official agenda for our meetings. All family members took turns being the chairperson and secretary.

You can use family meetings to discuss any conflict of needs, large or small, that arises between you and your children. Examples of items for discussion might include messes in the living room, use of the TV, or too much noise when Dad is taking a nap.

When discussing conflicts, it is important for family members to state their own needs or feelings in a nonjudgmental way and to listen respectfully as others express their own needs and feelings. Everyone can then brainstorm possible solutions and establish rules, if necessary. I recommend striving for consensus (100 percent agreement) before implementing a solution.

If your child fails to follow a rule that was set unanimously in a meeting, there is no need to nag him or impose a consequence. Instead, simply put the item on the agenda and discuss it again. You can suggest consequences, but these should only be implemented if everyone agrees to them in a family meeting.

After your children learn how family meetings work, they may begin to use the meeting format to bring up problems they have with each other (or with you!). This is a good sign that they have understood the benefits of the democratic process.

Family meetings are also useful for dividing up chores. You can make a list of chores and ask everyone in the family, including the adults, to choose which ones they would like to do. Children are surprisingly willing to cooperate when you invite them, in a nonthreatening way, to share the work involved in running a home and keeping it clean.

Although the democratic process can be time-consuming, it is worth the effort because it can be highly effective, and it teaches your child interpersonal conflict-resolution skills. Another advantage is that your child will be less likely to rebel during adolescence.

Tip 48

Teach responsibility.

Using rewards or artificially contrived consequences (punishments) is not an effective way to teach children responsibility. This approach often causes children to feel manipulated and controlled and may lead to rebellion. In an effort to avoid being too harsh or controlling, some parents go to the other extreme and repeatedly rescue their children from the natural consequences of their own behavior.

One problem with repeatedly rescuing your child is that you may deprive her of learning to take responsibility for herself. The tendency to over-rescue is at the root of a later, more damaging tendency, which is to "enable" a chemically dependent person by protecting her from the natural consequences of her addiction. The phenomenon of enabling can occur with any addictive behavior or bad habit. Another problem with over-rescuing is that this habit may cause you to sacrifice your own needs, and your child will feel anxious and insecure if she senses that you resent her.

Allowing your child to learn through *natural consequences* can be an effective way to encourage responsibility without either you or your child becoming resentful. Look for situations in which you might be doing too much for your child. Discuss the issue with her ahead of time and give her fair warning that you intend to change your behavior. Make sure she understands and agrees that you will no longer come to her rescue. Don't be rigid about this approach, however, and don't ever refuse to help your child if she is really suffering. The goal is *not* to make your child feel bad by "teaching her a lesson" but to encourage her to take responsibility for herself.

The following example illustrates the difference between artificial consequences, over-rescuing, and natural consequences.

Example: A six-year-old girl leaves her wet bathing suit and towel on the floor after her daily swim lesson.

- *Artificial consequence (child becomes resentful):* Father does not allow her to watch TV until she has hung them up.
- *Over-rescuing (parent becomes resentful):* Father hangs them up but becomes increasingly resentful of his daughter.
- *Natural consequence (nobody becomes resentful):* Father explains that he no longer wishes to hang them up and shows his daughter how to do it. If she chooses not to hang them up, she will find them still wet the next day.

Children who have learned to take responsibility for themselves will continue to act responsibly as they grow older because they understand that nobody will tell them what to do or rescue them from the consequences of their own actions. Because of this, they will be able to make wise decisions about drugs and sex.

Tip 49

Give an allowance, but don't use money as a reward.

Beginning at the age of six or seven years, you can give your child a regular allowance; the amount of money can depend on your child's age and your financial resources. Don't give too much, even if you are wealthy. The purpose of an allowance is for your child to learn about money and decision making.

To help your child become a good decision maker, avoid controlling how he spends his money. You can suggest that he save some of it, but he will learn best through his own experiences. If he spends all of his money impulsively for something that he later regrets, that will be a valuable learning experience. Later, when someone tries to sell drugs to him, he will know that purchasing immediate and temporary pleasures might not be the best way to spend his money.

Avoid giving or withholding money as a reward or punishment to control your child's behavior. Although it may be tempting to pay your child when he takes out the trash or withhold his allowance when he fights with his siblings, this kind of control will teach your child to do things for the wrong reasons. Rewarding your child for obedience will encourage him to pay attention only to his personal gain, and you will have no guarantee that he has learned any meaningful values or conflict-resolution skills.

As described in a tip for younger children (Tip 27), a better long-term goal is to teach your child to pay attention to the effects of his behavior on other people. Instead of paying your child to do chores, express your need for assistance and come to a mutual agreement in a family meeting. Instead of withholding your children's allowance when they fight with each other, teach them how to solve their conflicts nonviolently by listening to each other's feelings and needs.

Some parents wonder if they should pay their children for *extra* jobs around the home. If you would need to hire someone anyway, it might be okay to pay an older child to do the work. Be sure you understand, however, that paying your child will subtly but inevitably change his motivation for helping out. He will do so more in order to earn the money and less because of his desire to meet your need for assistance.

The risk of controlling your child's behavior through money or other rewards is that he will eventually outgrow your small rewards, yet still expect immediate personal gratification for the things he does. When looking elsewhere for more exciting rewards, he will see that drug dealers offer promises of immediate excitement in novel forms that make your rewards seem pale in comparison.

Tip 50

Don't be overprotective.

It is important to protect your child from all possible dangers. She should wear a bicycle helmet, use a seat belt, and learn basic safety rules for crossing a street or using an electrical appliance. She must stay away from fire and deep water, refuse gifts from strangers, and of course, avoid drugs.

The list of potential dangers can seem overwhelming, and many parents wonder how much protectiveness is too much. With my children, I struggled with questions like these: Should I tell my child not to run if I am afraid that she might fall? At what age is it safe for her to walk to a friend's home or take a bus alone? When can I let him use a sharp knife? Should I keep him away from children who are ill? And what's wrong with being overprotective anyway? Isn't it better to be safe than sorry?

The problem with being overprotective is that it may prevent your child from learning that there is a range of dangers, thereby diluting your message about the serious ones. If your child hears you say "Be careful" ten times a day to protect her from scraping a knee or spilling her milk, she will learn to shrug off your warnings. Later, when you tell her to be careful about drugs, she may think that the danger is no more serious than falling down or spilling milk. She will attribute your warnings to your overprotectiveness and fail to heed them.

I recommend saving the word "dangerous" and the expression "be careful" for life-threatening dangers such as deep or swift water, the edge of a cliff, fire, busy streets, dangerous tools, illnesses such as HIV, and of course, poisons and drugs. (This is a partial list of the many life-threatening dangers that exist.)

For less dangerous situations, you can avoid those specific terms while still protecting your child and giving her the information she needs to stay safe. You can say, for example, "I'm worried that you might cut yourself when you hold the knife that way. Let me show you a safer way to hold it." When appropriate, you can let your child learn from natural consequences. If she spills her milk or falls while running, she will learn to be more careful.

If you struggle with overprotectiveness, try to determine the origin of your fears. If your own parents were constantly worried about your safety, you might have internalized an exaggerated fear for yourself, which you then transferred to your own child. Sometimes our fears have their roots in a traumatic loss. If you have lost a child through death, it is only natural to be highly protective of your living child. However, if your fear and overprotectiveness are hampering your child's healthy development, it would be wise to take steps to heal from your previous loss.

Tip 51

Teach your child ways to get high without drugs.

The primary allure of drugs is their ability to produce an intensely pleasurable experience. This altered state of mind is called being high or stoned. However, other enjoyable activities, such as dancing, can also produce a feeling of being high, although it is generally milder than the chemical high produced by drugs. By teaching your child that it is possible to have pleasurable experiences without drugs, you will give him a precious gift that will reduce the allure of drugs for him.

Experiences in nature can be profoundly intense and moving. One of my most memorable experiences as a child was a two-day hike our family took in the Smoky Mountains of Tennessee when I was about eight years old. I remember climbing all day and finally reaching the top of the mountain, where we spent the night in a cabin. The next morning, we arose at 5 AM to view the sunrise. I was deeply moved by the beautiful pastel colors of that sunrise over the mountains, and this experience remains one of my most pleasant childhood memories to this day. Some people might call this a spiritual experience. It is not surprising to me that wilderness camps for drug-dependent and delinquent youth have a high success rate.

Strenuous exercise, too, can produce a natural high because of the release of endorphins in the brain. Children naturally love to run, and they usually seem quite cheerful after running, even though they might also be exhausted. Perhaps they are experiencing a natural high at those times. Some people achieve a similar state of euphoria through dance. Play a CD of your favorite music and dance with your child until you are both exhausted. Or take your child folk dancing.

Singing is another way to experience pleasure. One of my favorite activities is singing with others around a campfire. Performing for a live audience can also produce a natural high.

Don't forget the value of humor and laughter, which produces beneficial physiological effects. Be silly at times, by doing things wrong on purpose, or acting clumsy, stupid, or forgetful. Encourage your child to be silly as well. Your child will love it and will probably laugh. Amusement parks, water slides, and roller coasters also offer opportunities to laugh and experience the intense thrill of being alive.

After your child reaches the teenage years, he may become too embarrassed to engage in these kinds of activities with you. Now is the time to share these moments with your child and show him how to get high naturally, without drugs.

Tip 52

Build self-esteem through mastery and success.

High self-esteem is at the root of drug resistance. Children who feel good about themselves and their abilities are less likely to turn to drugs to fit in with a group or to mask feelings of inadequacy. In addition to helping your child succeed in school, you can enhance her self-esteem by creating situations at home in which she will be successful. Here are some suggestions.

- Give your child an animal or plant to take care of.
- Play games at which your child can win.
- Play cooperative games in which everyone wins.
- Get your child involved in a sport where she can measure her progress (for example, the time it takes to swim across a pool).
- Organize family recital nights in which each person plays a musical instrument, sings a song, or recites a poem.
- Put your child's drawings on your wall or refrigerator door.
- Help your child make presents for other family members.
- Give your child regular, age-appropriate chores. For example, let her sort the laundry.
- Ask for your child's help on special occasions. For example, let your child arrange flowers for a dinner party in your home.
- Teach your child a new skill, such as knitting.

It is important to acknowledge and appreciate your child's accomplishments, while avoiding criticisms if your child makes a mistake or fails to accomplish something. Let her know that mistakes are a normal part of learning.

There is no need for external rewards because the feeling of mastery should be its own reward. Praise with value judgments is not helpful either. When my children accomplished something, I avoided saying, "Good job," because I didn't want them to become dependent on my approval. Furthermore, I worried that the word "good" would set up an expectation of perfection. The opposite of good is bad, so how would they feel if they made a mistake the next time? An enthusiastic, "You did it!" or a heartfelt word of thanks will help your child feel recognized and appreciated. Another alternative to saying "good" is to give specific feedback: "I see five different colors in your drawing," or "Wow! That's the farthest I've ever seen you swim!"

Your confidence and encouragement will give your child the support she needs to develop good self-esteem by mastering increasingly difficult tasks.

Tip 53

Minimize competition in sports and games.

There is nothing wrong with friendly competition that motivates people to develop their skills, measure themselves against others, and perform at high levels. However, if losing a game causes a person to feel worthless or depressed, competition has gone too far. Boys whose self-esteem is linked to their athletic ability are at risk for taking steroids to enhance their strength or endurance. Young people of both sexes sometimes use stimulants or other drugs to increase their alertness, stamina, or strength during competitive sports.

One thing you can do to counter the problems inherent in competitive sports and games is to de-emphasize the importance of winning. Teach your child that the major purpose of sports is to make friends, get some exercise, and have fun. Whether your child wins or loses a game should not be important to you. When your child wins a game or competition, share his pleasure. If he loses, accept his disappointment, but do not convey your own disappointment in his performance, even if you think he could have done better. Say, for example, "You seem pretty upset about the soccer game. It's disappointing to lose after all that practicing you did. I hope you had fun anyway."

To create a balance in your child's life, you can teach him cooperative sports and games. Look for books describing enjoyable games that do not involve winning or losing. I always led cooperative games at my children's birthday parties, and all the children had a great time. Nobody was bothered by the fact that there were no winners because I gave prizes to everyone.

There are also cooperative indoor games and table games, and you can modify many traditional competitive games so they become cooperative.

Brain scans of people playing strategy games reveal that they use different parts of their brain depending on whether they are instructed to play cooperatively or competitively. A specific part of the brain (the orbitofrontal cortex) is activated while playing a game cooperatively, but not when playing competitively. This part of the brain is known to be involved in socially rewarding activities, implying that cooperative games are inherently rewarding and pleasurable. The psychological satisfaction that we experience after reaching a common goal through interaction with someone else is different from the satisfaction of winning a competitive game. Perhaps we could even use cooperative games to produce a natural high!

By teaching your child cooperative games and by minimizing the importance of winning competitive ones, you will teach him a drug-free way to have fun with friends and reduce his risk of taking dangerous drugs as a teenager to enhance his athletic abilities.

Tip 54

Avoid negative comments about your child's weight
or appearance.

Children need to grow up with a good self-image. Feelings of
unattractiveness can lower their self-esteem and increase their
risk of using drugs to feel accepted by others. It is therefore
important to help your child feel attractive.

Overweight girls are at especially high risk for drug abuse
because substances such as nicotine, stimulants (including
Ritalin), and cocaine can help them lose weight by curbing
their appetite. If your child is overweight, avoid commenting
on this fact. Your child already knows that she is overweight,
and she may even be getting teased about it at school.

You can help your overweight child by providing wholesome
food and encouraging healthy eating habits, while refraining
from controlling your child's diet. It is not helpful to give warnings or reminders such as: "If you eat so much cake, you're
going to get so fat that nobody will want to play with you," or
"If you want to be attractive, you had better stop eating so
many chips. You know how fattening they are."

If your child continuously overeats, consider the possible
contribution of stress toward the problem. Eating addictions
are similar to drug addictions because they are both inappropriate coping mechanisms. Help her find ways to minimize
stress, and allow her to express her emotions so she won't
need to repress painful feelings by overeating. You can accomplish this goal without criticizing your child, nagging her about
her eating habits, or implying that her weight devalues her as
a person.

You can further help your overweight child by encouraging plenty of exercise and helping her feel good about her body through physical abilities such as sports or dance. You can also help her find attractive clothes to wear that do not draw attention to her weight.

Avoid comparing your children to each other. Sometimes parents unknowingly criticize their children by making comments such as, "Mary is our little scholar and Susie is our little movie star," implying that Susie is more attractive than Mary. Comparisons such as these can damage both children's self-esteem.

If you are the mother of a daughter, try to be a good role model by avoiding negative comments about your own weight or body proportions in front of her. She may become overly self-conscious because of you or feel indirectly criticized if she looks like you.

If your child does not fit the cultural norm of physical beauty because of unusual facial features or a disability, do everything you can to help her feel attractive and to let her know that *you* find her attractive. Don't ever tell your child, directly or indirectly, that she is unattractive.

A word of caution: Consult a doctor if your child is overweight or underweight, or if you suspect an eating disorder.

Tip 55

Don't tell your child that he is too sensitive.

Sensitivity is an inborn temperament trait, and 15 to 20 percent of children of both sexes are born with a highly sensitive nature. These children are more easily stressed and overstimulated than others.

Don't ever tell your child that he is "too sensitive." In my workshops for parents, I sometimes ask the participants to raise their hand if their parents ever told them they were too sensitive. Often, as many as half the participants raise their hand, and many are relieved to see that others experienced the same criticism.

If you have a highly sensitive son, you may fear that he lacks the resilience necessary for coping in a competitive and tough world. But sensitivity is a wonderful asset, and the world needs sensitive men. Highly sensitive boys who have been made to feel they should be aggressive and hide their feelings are at risk for abusing drugs later on as a way to function in a world that often overwhelms them. They may even take drugs so they can act and feel like other boys. So try to accept and enjoy your son's sensitive, gentle nature rather than attempt to change him to fit the cultural norm for male behavior.

If you have a highly sensitive child of either sex, you will need to be especially patient and willing to listen to his painful feelings. Highly sensitive children feel everything more intensely than other children, and they may need to cry more frequently. So be prepared for lots of crying about events that may seem trivial to you. Your child is not overreacting by crying so much; he is simply releasing painful emotions in a healthy way.

You can help your sensitive child by protecting him from stress and overstimulation. Don't schedule too many activities for him. Allow him to have plenty of time in which to relax. Don't let him watch frightening movies or read books that may be too intense for him. Don't expect him to enjoy surprises or big parties. Prepare him carefully for major changes, and even for transitions from one activity to another. Keep your home environment peaceful.

Sensitive children are cautious and slow to warm up to people they don't know, so others often describe them as shy. Don't expect your sensitive child to have lots of friends. Encourage him to find one or two good friends, and don't push him into social situations for which he might not be ready. Shy children are at risk for taking drugs such as marijuana or alcohol later on as a way to relax and overcome social inhibitions.

By understanding your child's sensitive nature rather than trying to change it, you will help him accept himself, learn to minimize stress, and find his place in the world without resorting to drugs in order to cope with stressful situations.

Tip 56

Be aware of sexist stereotypes and oppression for girls.

Both boys and girls suffer from sexual stereotyping, and they feel the effects very early in life. These stereotypes can cause emotional stress and pressure to conform, which can, in turn, contribute to specific patterns of drug abuse during adolescence.

In the case of girls, the major pressure is to be physically attractive in order to please the other sex. Our culture conveys this expectation to girls by promoting clothing that is often impractical and hampers freedom of movement, dolls with fancy clothing and hair styles, and endless advertisements for beauty aids. Girls as young as eight years of age now feel that they must dress in the latest fashion, and ten- to twelve-year-olds want to wear makeup.

An especially damaging cultural myth is that of equating beauty with thinness, which is promoted by the portrayal of unnaturally thin women in women's magazines, advertisements, movies, and television programs. It is not surprising that many girls succumb to this myth by going on a diet as early as the age of ten. Carried to an extreme, this tendency can lead to eating disorders during adolescence (anorexia or bulimia). There is a growing epidemic of adolescent eating disorders, primarily in girls. In order to lose weight, girls are at risk for taking drugs that curb their appetite. These drugs are primarily nicotine (tobacco), methamphetamine, Ritalin, and cocaine.

Our culture also discourages girls from developing their skills in mathematics and science, expecting them instead to enter into the helping professions such as teaching or nursing.

This expectation puts pressure on girls who are attracted to the sciences because they feel different. Until the age of twelve years, girls perform as well as boys in math and science, but after that age, their performance and interest in these subjects decline. This decline is probably the direct result of cultural expectations.

Because of these various pressures, girls who do not fit the cultural norm for beauty or who have interests that differ from cultural expectations are often desperate to fit in with their peers during adolescence. If their peer group experiments with drugs, these girls will be vulnerable to going along with the group.

You cannot counteract all of these cultural influences on your daughter, but you can give her your unconditional love and support. Increase her resilience and self-esteem by letting her know that physical beauty comes in all shapes and sizes. Avoid buying fashion clothing for her before she requests it, and support her interests and skills, whatever they are. Let her know that she can pursue any career she chooses, and encourage her to be strong and independent. A girl who feels her parents' support for having interests that differ from the cultural norm will feel comfortable being a nonconformist, and this will strengthen her against peer influences to use drugs.

Tip 57

Be aware of sexist stereotypes and oppression for boys.

Both boys and girls suffer from sexual stereotyping, but it manifests itself differently for the two sexes. Our culture expects boys to be brave, independent, strong, and unfeeling. The typical man portrayed in the movies or on TV is one who can fight but who cannot communicate or feel tender emotions. Feelings of sadness, fear, compassion, or genuine love (as opposed to sexual passion) are considered a sign of weakness. Some men do not even feel safe enough to admit physical pain when they are injured. This stereotype is slowly changing, as some politicians and sports heroes are becoming courageous enough to cry in public. But the image of the strong, unfeeling man is still an influential part of our culture.

Because of this expectation for acceptable male behavior, little boys often struggle with their strong emotions. When they feel sad or frightened, they fear that others will tease them for being too weak or "girlish" if they cry. This repression of painful emotions can lead to excessive emotional baggage when they reach adolescence, with the tendency to use drugs to feel better. Alcohol is especially effective in blunting painful emotions.

To counteract this cultural stereotype of unfeeling men, it is vital to encourage your son to express his emotions. I have emphasized repeatedly throughout this book the importance of allowing your children to cry. If you find it more difficult to accept your son's crying than your daughter's, take a moment to examine your attitude toward men and emotions. What kind of male role models did you have as a child? Are you afraid that your son will be too weak to survive in a competitive world? If you are a man, how did your parents respond when you cried? Remember that the world needs compassionate men who are aware of their emotions and who can cry when they need to.

You can also counteract the cultural expectation for men to be independent. Too often, we parents push our sons away from us too soon, thinking that they don't need us any more. But the attachment needs of boys are just as strong as those of girls. Give your son as much physical affection as you would give a daughter the same age. Don't push him to become independent, and find ways to stay connected to him as he grows older. Your continuing interest and affection may be the most important inoculation you can give him against drugs.

Tip 58

Take action if your child is being bullied or victimized.

There are several reasons why being victimized or bullied can put children at risk for taking drugs. First, children who are bullied have a desperate need to be accepted, and this need makes them more vulnerable to conformity when their peers use drugs. Second, bullies sometimes force younger children to obtain illegal drugs for them, thereby putting the bullied children into direct contact with the drug scene. Third, being bullied causes stress, which can lead to drug abuse.

Bullying can range from mild teasing to physical assault. The children who become bullies usually have low self-esteem and have been victimized themselves by other children, older siblings, or their parents. They pick on children who appear to be easy targets, and any difference can serve as a pretext, such as clothing, skin color, disability, height, weight (especially obesity), early breast development in girls, speech defect, foreign accent, shyness, awkwardness, freckles, or crooked teeth.

If you suspect that your child is being bullied at school, it is important to discuss this with her and help her figure out how to handle the bully. Let her know that you are willing to talk with her teacher or principal. It is the responsibility of schools to keep children safe, so if your child does not feel safe at school, it is important to let the school staff know. Be sure to take action immediately if your child has been physically harmed or has received a serious threat.

Many schools now recognize the problem of bullying and have established a zero tolerance level for it. Bullies are identified and offered the help they need. If necessary, they are moved to another educational setting. My children's school had a preventive program. Older children were paired up with younger children and met with them several times during the year, reading to them, doing a supervised craft project, or helping them with schoolwork. This "little buddy" system gave each new child at the school an older playground ally, and it helped the older children feel protective and nurturing toward the younger ones. Programs such as these can reduce the frequency of bullying.

If the school is unable or unwilling to address the problem, and your child is afraid to go to school or shows symptoms of stress (such as frequent tantrums, nightmares, or phobias), you might have to remove your child from the school, at least temporarily. Be sure to write a letter to your child's teacher and send copies to the school principal and superintendent. Explain that the reason for your child's absence is to protect her physical or mental health.

Tip 59

Get professional help if your child has experienced trauma.

Sometimes an overwhelmingly stressful or life-threatening event occurs, which shatters a child's core sense of safety. Such events are called traumas. Emotional traumas like these can have a long-term negative impact on your child, even if they occurred during infancy:

- Physical or sexual abuse
- Death of a family member or close friend
- Prolonged separation from parents
- Parental divorce
- Life-threatening illness
- Serious accident
- Surgery or hospitalization
- Witnessing violence to others
- Natural disasters (floods, fires, earthquakes, hurricanes)
- Terrorism or war

Children who are suffering from trauma often feel anxious, insecure, confused, depressed, guilty, or angry. Post-traumatic behavioral symptoms can be fairly mild or obvious and severe. (See Tip 61.) In my consulting experience, I have found that parents and professionals often overlook the impact of emotional trauma as a possible cause of annoying behaviors such as hyperactivity, impulsivity, aggression, inability to concentrate, obnoxiousness, or defiance.

Love and the passage of time are not always sufficient for children to heal from trauma. If your child has experienced any traumatic events, *even if you have not noticed any alarming symptoms,* I highly recommend that you seek professional help because symptoms of early trauma can surface later in life, and traumatized children are at high risk for later substance abuse and depression.

Begin by finding support for yourself because you will need to be in good shape to help your child. If you are experiencing guilt, grief, fear, or anger, your child will be less able to heal effectively. You can seek family therapy or parenting guidance from professionals familiar with childhood trauma. Look for individual psychotherapy, group therapy, or a support group for your child. Try to find a professional with knowledge and experience in childhood trauma. The field of clinical psychology has developed numerous effective approaches for helping traumatized children and their families.

Tip 60

Allow your child to grieve following a loss.

The mother of a thirteen-year-old girl consulted with me because her daughter was out of control and beginning to experiment with drugs. After some questioning, I learned that the father had died when the girl was ten years old and that the mother-daughter relationship had been strained ever since his death. The girl never spoke about her father. When I suggested to the mother that perhaps her daughter had not fully grieved the loss, it made sense to her. So together we discussed steps she could take to help her daughter heal from the trauma, such as sharing memories of the father, looking at photos, and encouraging the girl to cry. A month later, the mother contacted me to say that my advice had helped her reconnect with her daughter, and the girl's problems had disappeared.

The death of a parent is one of the most traumatic experiences a child can encounter. Sometimes children sense the fragility of the remaining parent and try to protect that parent by not revealing the extent of their grief. But they do this at a great cost to their emotional well-being. Unresolved grief, which is carried into the early adolescent years, can then become a contributing factor to behavior problems and drug abuse.

If the girl in the above example had seen a therapist immediately after her father's death, or if the mother and daughter had gone into therapy together, the problems at age thirteen might not have occurred. Luckily, this mother recognized the problem early enough so that she was able to solve it quite easily.

When your child has been traumatized by the death of someone close, she will not heal completely unless she is allowed to cry, possibly for many hours over a period of weeks or months. When my father was a child, his mother died, and his relatives told him that he shouldn't cry because his mother had gone to heaven. This lack of support for his natural urge to cry may have been a significant factor contributing to my father's lifelong depression.

The death of a grandparent or other relative can also be highly traumatic. Even the death of another child's parent or grandparent can traumatize your child. When my daughter was seven years old, the mother of a girl in her class committed suicide. This tragic event had a huge impact on all the children, some of whom developed separation anxiety and other fears. The teacher arranged for a psychologist to meet with the class so the children could ask questions and share their feelings.

Don't underestimate the impact of the loss of a pet. If your child's cat or dog dies, allow her to grieve fully. The extent of your child's grief will be related to her emotional attachment to the animal, so don't accuse your child of overreacting, even if the animal was only a goldfish or a lizard.

Tip 61

Look for warning signs of serious emotional problems.

Children with serious emotional problems are at risk for taking drugs to feel better as soon as drugs become available to them. These ten warning signs are possible indicators of severe emotional problems.

- Is preoccupied with death, blood, and gore
- Talks about wanting to die
- Purposely injures himself or is unusually accident-prone
- Sets fires, kills animals, hurts other children, damages property
- Repeatedly lies or steals
- Never cries, is withdrawn, passive, or unemotional
- Regresses to earlier stages of development for more than a month (for example, wets his pants)
- Has frequent nightmares (for more than a month)
- Has intense phobias that interfere with normal functioning (for more than a month)
- Is precociously preoccupied by sex, beyond mere curiosity (for example, acts seductively or draws pictures of sex organs)

Don't worry about occasional behaviors that fit in one of these categories. For example, if your child sometimes has a nightmare or hits his brother, there is no need to be overly concerned. Likewise, there is nothing to worry about if your child wants to dress up as a vampire or if he goes through a period of being afraid to sleep alone. It's only when these behaviors are extreme and repetitive that you should consider that your child may have a serious emotional problem.

It won't help to ignore the above symptoms with the hope that they will disappear by themselves. These behaviors usually have their origin in some form of emotional trauma, even though you may not be aware of any major trauma in your child's life. Sometimes parents fail to realize that their child is troubled, and the child doesn't receive the help he needs. They may think that these behaviors are simply "discipline" problems or a reflection of their child's personality. However, children who display these various symptoms are usually struggling with intense emotions and are at *very high risk* for drug abuse, violent or suicidal behavior, eating disorders, and major depression.

If your child displays these warning signs, find help for him now, before it is too late. First consult a pediatrician to check for possible medical causes. Then look for a clinical psychologist or counselor. Severely disturbed children can benefit from individual or family therapy, but don't expect professionals to "fix" your child without your help. With information and guidance, you can play a major role in your child's recovery.

Tip 62

Give your child information about drugs.

Some children begin taking drugs before the age of twelve. It is therefore wise to give your child information about the various psychoactive drugs around the age of eight or nine so she will know what she might encounter. Even if your child's school has a drug-education program, it is also beneficial for her to hear this information directly from you.

Inform yourself about the appearance, popular names, side effects, and corresponding paraphernalia of the various drugs that are abused. Children and teenagers today have access to a wide variety of potent, addictive, and dangerous substances. Remember that some of the current drugs are more potent today than in the past, and new synthetic drugs are constantly being created.

A good way to begin the discussion is by reading a book with your child on the topic of drugs. There are many excellent books on this topic, including ones written specifically for children. (See Resources.) In addition, you can make use of times when the topic arises naturally in the news or during conversations with your child.

The major categories of psychoactive drugs include the following:

- Caffeine (coffee, chocolate, tea, soft drinks)
- Alcohol
- Nicotine (tobacco)
- Marijuana and hashish

- Inhalants (hair spray, glue, paint thinner, nitrous oxide, etc.)
- Amphetamines, methamphetamine, and prescription stimulants
- Cocaine
- LSD and other hallucinogens (mescaline, psilocybin)
- Ecstasy and other synthetic drugs (PCP, GHB, etc.)
- Opiates (opium, morphine, heroin, and opiate-based prescription painkillers)
- Prescription tranquilizers (barbiturates, benzodiazepines)
- Prescription antidepressants
- Steroids
- Over-the-counter drugs (cough syrup, antihistamines, decongestants)

Teach your child what these various drugs look like and what the psychological and physical effects are. A common mistake is to tell children all the bad things about drugs without admitting the basic fact that *drugs make people feel good and can make troubles seem to vanish.* When your child later discovers the pleasant effects of drugs, she may feel betrayed if you withheld this information. She might then dismiss all the other information you gave her. So don't be afraid to tell your child about the pleasant effects of drugs.

However, your child also needs to know that many drugs are highly addictive and that a single dose of certain drugs or a combination of drugs can be deadly. The fact that a friend has taken a drug with no ill effects does not make it safe, because drugs can affect people in different ways. Tell your child that drugs can damage her brain and other parts of her body. She should not trust anybody, not even a friend, who offers her a substance to swallow other than food or a nonalcoholic drink. In addition, she should never inhale, sniff, snort, or inject *anything*. The only exception to these rules is medication prescribed by a doctor for her. She should never take someone else's medicine. Tell her that even over-the-counter cold remedies, such as cough syrup, can be deadly in large quantities.

Tip 63

Teach your child the legal consequences of using drugs.

In addition to learning about the various drugs, your child also needs to know that some drugs are legal while others are illegal. The list of illegal drugs has changed over the years and is not the same in all countries. State, country, and international authorities use a variety of methods to control the sale of dangerous substances. Some drugs are restricted to people over a certain age, such as alcohol in the United States, while others are illegal for everybody. Some drugs can be obtained only with a doctor's prescription. Explain to your child that these laws were established to keep people safe.

Let your child know which drugs are illegal and what the legal consequences are for possessing or selling them. Tell him that illegal substances found in your home or car will put *you* in legal jeopardy. Tell your child that it's a crime to possess or sell drugs whether you get caught or not, just as going through a red light is against the law even when no policeman is present.

A possible source of confusion is prescription drugs, so don't forget to mention that it is illegal to resell a prescription drug, even though the drug itself was obtained legally. Two kinds of prescription drugs commonly resold illegally are stimulants (such as Ritalin) and opiate-based painkillers.

Be sure to include information about the legal consequences of driving while intoxicated, even though it will be many years before your child has a driver's license. Explain to your child that alcohol and drugs can be detected in the blood, urine, or breath.

If you know of someone who was arrested for using, possessing, or selling a psychoactive drug, share that information with your child, and explain how it changed the person's life. If you do not know of anyone, you can wait for such an event to be reported in the news.

The important thing for your child to learn is that there are serious consequences for possessing or selling certain substances. However, don't forget to emphasize also that *all psychoactive drugs can be abused and have health risks, whether they are legal or not.*

By twelve years of age, your child should be familiar not only with the appearance, effects, and dangers of the various kinds of drugs but also with the legal consequences for possessing or selling them.

Tip 64

Teach your child media and consumer awareness.

Our culture bombards us with positive messages about drugs. Legal drugs such as tobacco and alcohol are advertised on TV, the radio, the Internet, in magazines, on posters, and at sports events. These ads attempt to make smoking and drinking look glamorous and sexy. The cigarette industry is increasingly directing its ads at young people. Further influence comes from the fact that smoking and drinking are frequently portrayed in movies in conjunction with love scenes. An analysis of the most successful teen-centered films revealed that substance use was portrayed as being common and risk free.

Remind your child that companies in a free market economy must convince consumers to buy their products in order to make a profit and stay in business. Explain that these companies are interested only in making money, not in enhancing people's health. Make sure your child understands that the people portrayed in the ads have been paid huge sums of money. An effective way to teach this information is to make use of "teachable moments" in everyday life. For example, if you see a cigarette ad that uses a woman's photo, you can say, "I wonder how much that woman was paid to have her photo taken."

Teach your child also to be aware of the profit motive of pharmaceutical companies. A major part of the marketing campaign for psychiatric drugs is to convince people that specific medications are essential for solving their emotional problems. While psychiatric drugs may benefit some people some of the time, we need to counteract the pervasive assumption that we can cure *all* of our emotional problems by taking a pill. When we accept that assumption, it is all too easy to justify the consumption of illegal drugs.

When evaluating statements about legal drugs, teach your child always to check the source of funding. If the funding came from a beer manufacturer, a tobacco company, or a pharmaceutical company, that fact should be taken into account. Also tell your child that scientific research and opinion polls can be misrepresented and distorted and that the Internet is not always a source of reliable information.

This information will help your child develop a healthy skepticism. If she learns this lesson well, she will be better armed to resist peer pressure to take drugs. More specifically, she will think twice before believing a drug dealer who tells her that a street drug is safe. Your child will know that this information is biased by the dealer's desire to make a profit. She will also resist being influenced by glamorous images of legal drugs.

Chapter 5

Ages 12 to 18

Tip 65

Spend regular one-on-one time with your teen.

A distraught mother once consulted with me about her seventeen-year-old son who was "in trouble with drugs." She had to make an important decision about whether to send him to an in-patient treatment program against his will. After his eighteenth birthday (in three months) she would no longer have the legal right to do so. I asked her several questions and learned that the only drug her son had tried was marijuana, but she was worried that he would progress to other drugs, as sometimes happens. I asked her what he liked to do (other than smoke marijuana), and she replied that he enjoyed hiking but that they hadn't done much together as a family recently. My advice? "Go hiking with him," I said. She later thanked me for reminding her that she could play an important role in turning her son's life around.

What is it about our culture that makes it necessary for professionals to tell parents to spend more time with their kids? I don't blame the mother in this example because part of the fault lies with us professionals. In making great efforts to avoid blaming parents for their children's problems, we absolve parents of all responsibility. It is no surprise, then, that parents often fail to realize that they are important in their children's lives and can be part of the solution.

Don't let your child's growing independence deceive you into thinking that he no longer needs you. Even though he doesn't say, "Mommy, play with me," he still needs your attention. Suggest activities that you both enjoy, whether it's hiking, swimming, shopping, or going to a movie. Don't underestimate the importance of simple conversation. You can spend high-quality time together just staying home and talking.

Encourage conversation with your teen after school by asking him how his day went. If you ask a general question such as "How was school?" you are likely to obtain a short answer such as "Fine." More specific questions, based on previous information your teen has given you, are likely to yield a longer reply. Try asking questions like, "You were worried about that history test this morning. How did it go?" or "Is your friend still sick with the flu?" You teen will be pleased that you remembered those details about his life.

If your teen is reluctant to spend time with you or even talk with you, the most likely reason is that you have not listened well to him in the past or have used a punitive approach to discipline. Other tips in this book will help you improve your communication and discipline skills.

To sum up this basic tip for drug resistance: Your teen needs you to be interested in his life and available to spend time with him. Sometimes it's as simple as that.

Tip 66

Do things together as a family.

In addition to spending individual time with your teen, it's important to do things together as a family because family activities foster a sense of connection. Interestingly, teens whose families frequently eat dinner together are less likely to abuse drugs.

As your child grows older, she will naturally want to spend more time with her friends and less time with the family. Explain to your teen that you welcome her participation in family activities. However, don't *force* your teen to participate. Instead, make the activity attractive so she will *want* to participate. For example, keep the conversation at the dinner table interesting by discussing topics that are relevant to her life.

Suggestions for family activities include the following:

- Eat meals together. Try to eat at least one meal a day together as a family.
- Play games or make music. Games and music are wonderful ways to enjoy each other's company.
- Attend movies, concerts, or plays. You can also rent videos or DVDs and watch them together as a family.
- Go on family outings or trips. Traveling as a family can be a wonderful bonding experience. If you have limited financial resources, choose low-cost activities such as hiking, camping trips, or visiting relatives in another city.
- Work on family projects. Working toward a common goal is an excellent way to build family cohesiveness. Examples of projects are baking cookies, painting a room, or creating a photo album for grandma's birthday.

- Maintain family traditions. Rituals and traditions are important because they provide predictability and structure, and the symbols help mark holidays and transitions in meaningful ways. Continue to maintain the traditions you established when your child was younger.

If your teen never wants to do anything with the family, try to determine the reason. Perhaps you nag, yell, criticize, or give unwanted advice. If you use punitive discipline, your teen will be more likely to avoid family activities. Do you frequently argue with your partner? Is there unresolved sibling rivalry? Are younger children getting all your attention? Are you giving your teen too many responsibilities, such as expecting her to baby-sit younger siblings?

If you make family life pleasant and agreeable for your teen, she will want to join in, and she will benefit from the feeling of security. This connection to the family will help to inoculate her against drugs.

Tip 67

Don't pressure your child to grow up too soon.

Teens have mixed, and sometimes painful, feelings about growing up, and these stresses are related in complex ways to drug abuse. On the one hand, teens experiment with drugs because it makes them feel grown up. Some children experience their first cigarette or first alcoholic drink almost as a rite of passage into the adult world. On the other hand, drugs can help teens avoid the painful feelings and responsibilities inherent in becoming an adult, especially when they are being pressured to succeed in school, sports, or other activities.

The drug Ecstasy involves an entire culture of parties with childhood symbols such as colorful clothing, teddy bears, and lollipops. It's as if the teens who use this drug are nostalgic about their childhood and reluctant to give it up.

Between twelve and fifteen years of age children vacillate between childhood and adolescence, and their interests are not necessarily related to their sexual maturity. Your thirteen-year-old daughter may still enjoy playing with dolls even though she began menstruating at the age of eleven. Your fourteen-year-old son may still enjoy childhood board games even though he has a bass voice. There is nothing wrong with encouraging these childhood interests because your child will grow up when she is ready to do so. So don't force your child to give away childhood toys, books, games, dolls, and stuffed animals.

It's reasonable to expect your teen to help at home from time to time and to assume more responsibilities as he grows older. But don't burden your teen with too many responsibilities, such as frequently taking care of younger siblings or cooking meals for the family.

Another way we force children to grow up too soon is when we expect them to get a job and earn money. If your teen wants a job to earn some money, or if your family is struggling financially, then it makes sense for him to work. However, some parents pressure their teens to hold a part-time job not only during the summer holidays but also during the school year, thinking it will give their teens valuable experience or keep them out of trouble. Although some teens might benefit from this experience, pressure to work while going to school can also lead to unnecessary stress.

It's normal for teens to act childish one day and want to be treated like an adult the next day. This can be confusing for parents. Don't expect your child to always act like an adult; let him be silly, have fun, and laugh. Let him know, too, that it's okay for him to cry, even though he might be taller than you are. He needs to know that you will always accept his emotions, whatever they are.

By letting your teen grow up at his own pace, you will help him become a mature and responsible adult and strengthen his drug resistance.

Tip 68

Remember that fathers are important.

A strong connection to at least one loving parent helps to inoculate children against drugs. However, a connection to two parents is even better. Both mothers and fathers can play an important role in helping teens stay away from drugs.

Many children do not have their fathers present in their lives. The reasons for this lack of fathering include separation or divorce, alcoholism or drug addiction, incarceration, military deployment, or death. Some women choose to become single mothers, and lesbian couples sometimes adopt a child or choose to conceive through artificial insemination.

Whatever the reason for a father-absent home, realize that both boys and girls benefit from having a close male role model involved in their lives. Boys, especially, need a male role model. If your son's father is unavailable or unwilling to be involved in his son's life, try to find another man to be a mentor or companion for your son. Perhaps an uncle, grandfather, or family friend can spend time with him, even if it's only playing basketball on Saturday afternoons.

If you are a father reading this, think of ways that you can become more involved in your child's life, and don't underestimate your importance. Is anything getting in the way of your being more involved? Can you change your work hours to better accommodate your child's needs for your attention? If you do not feel close to your child, take time to explore your relationship with your own father. Did he live with you when you were the same age as your child? Did he help support the family? What pleasant or painful memories do you have of him?

What did you especially enjoy doing with him? Was he a strict disciplinarian? What do you wish he had done differently? What kind of relationship do you have with him now (if he is alive)? How do you want to be like him? How do you want to be different?

If your father was absent during your adolescent years, it will be difficult for you to know how to be a father to teenage children because you had no role model. If he was a strict disciplinarian, you might find it difficult to be tender and compassionate with your children. Don't be hard on yourself if you make mistakes. Keep trying to be a better father, and remember that you are vitally important for your child's healthy emotional development.

Tip 69

Provide adequate supervision.

An important factor in preventing drug use by teens is to supervise them adequately. The following tips will help you accomplish this goal.

- *Know where your teen is.* Explain to your teen that family members need to know where the others are for safety and help in times of need. Let your teen know where you are at all times, and expect him to do likewise. Even if your teen has a cell phone, you need to know where he is. It's not that you don't trust your child. It's a matter of safety for you to know his location.

- *Make your home attractive for teens.* By creating a teen-friendly home, you will encourage your teen to spend time at home, where you can easily supervise him and his friends. Provide equipment for playing CDs, DVDs, and video games. Keep your refrigerator and pantry well stocked with healthy snacks. If you have the room, obtain a ping-pong or pool table or install an outdoor basketball hoop. Avoid doing or saying something that might embarrass your teen in front of his friends.

- *Supervise all social events in your home.* Try to be home when your teen invites friends over for socializing. Your presence is especially important during evening parties, although you do not actually have to be present in the room. You can make a friendly appearance and then disappear into a back room. If your teen says, "Don't you trust us?" you can explain that you do trust him but that you did not raise his friends, and you have no reason to trust that they will always avoid drugs. Make it clear that you will not tolerate any drugs or violence in your home and that you will call the police if necessary.

- *Become acquainted with the parents of your teen's friends.* If you don't already know the parents of your teen's friends, try to find ways to meet them. You can discuss with them the need for supervision and request that an adult always be present during parties at their homes. You will then be reassured that social events are properly supervised.

- *Let your teen know that you are available, twenty-four hours a day, to fetch him by car.* Your teen needs to know that he can rely on you to pick him up by car at any time of the day or night and that you will do so without probing or criticizing him. Let him know that he should not hesitate to call you if he is in trouble in any way or just needs a ride home (perhaps to avoid riding with an intoxicated driver). When your teen is out in the evening, it's wise to stay up until he returns home or sleep next to a telephone.

Tip 70

Respect your teen's privacy.

During the adolescent years, it is vital to maintain a good, trusting relationship with your child. One way to accomplish this goal is to respect your child's need for privacy. Somewhat paradoxically, the less you probe or snoop, the more likely your teen will be to share her personal life with you.

This openness and trust between the two of you will be useful when discussing topics related to sex or drugs. Also, by avoiding too much probing into your teen's personal life, she will be more likely to respect your genuine need to know where she is at all times.

- *Give your teen her own room.* It's important for teens to have a private room where they can do as they wish and which they can decorate as they choose. If your teen must share a room with a sibling, install a partition so that each child will have his or her own private space. Tell your teen that you will not enter her room without her permission, unless you have concerns about safety issues such as fire hazards or illegal drugs.
- *Don't look at private items.* Don't read your teen's diary, letters, or e-mail. It's none of your business, no matter how curious you are. Respect your teen's privacy just as you would respect the privacy of a guest in your home.
- *Don't ask probing questions.* Don't ask questions about your teen's personal life, and avoid mentioning sensitive topics to her. For example, if you suspect that your daughter has a crush on a boy, there is no need to men-

tion your suspicions or ask her about it. Let her take the initiative to tell you about it if she wishes, and don't be surprised if she never mentions it.

- *Respect confidentiality.* If your teen has revealed something of a personal nature to you, don't tell it to other people, even close family members, without her permission. For example, if your daughter has talked to you about a boy that seems interested in her, request her permission before conveying this information to your spouse.
- *Don't listen to phone calls.* It goes without saying that you should not listen in when your teen is on the phone. If she is making a phone call from her room, don't stand near the door to listen. Avoid the temptation to ask her about personal telephone conversations.
- *Don't ever restrict privacy as a punishment.* (In fact, don't use any punishment at all.) I have heard of a parent taking off the door to a teen's room as a punishment. Needless to say, such punishment will anger and alienate your teen. Restricting phone calls is another cruel form of punishment. (See Tips 47 and 73 for suggestions of ways to solve conflicts without punishment.)

Tip 71

Listen, listen, listen.

Teenagers frequently complain that their parents don't listen and don't understand. This lack of good communication can lead to a feeling of disconnection from parents, which can put teens at risk for using drugs as a way of coping with problems. Teens who have good communication with their parents are less likely to use drugs.

Good listening involves reflecting back your teen's feelings so he feels fully heard. This is called "active listening" or "reflective listening." Parents sometimes find it difficult to listen well to their teenage children. The four major mistakes are advising, blaming, consoling, and rescuing.

The example below illustrates these four mistakes. It is followed by an example of helpful listening, which is an actual transcript of a conversation between a parent and teenager.

David (age 15, angry): I *hate* my basketball coach! He never lets me play. Only the best kids get to play in the games. All I do is sit on the sidelines.

Examples of unhelpful listening:

Advising: You should tell your coach how you feel. You've got to learn to speak up for yourself.

Blaming: What do you expect? Some of those kids have been playing basketball since they were seven years old. You never wanted to join a team when you were younger.

Consoling: I'm sure you'll improve with practice. Be patient, it takes time. Your coach just hasn't seen your potential yet.

Rescuing: I'll have a talk with your coach. It doesn't sound fair to me. That's no way to treat an eager young basketball player like you.

Example of helpful listening:

Mother: It sounds like you're pretty angry at that coach, and you're feeling left out.

David: Yeah! I thought basketball would be fun. All they're interested in is winning.

Mother: You were looking forward to being on a real team, and now you're disappointed because it's so competitive.

David: Maybe team sports isn't for me. I like basketball, but I guess I'm just not that competitive. I prefer to shoot baskets with my friends on the weekend. I'll stay on the team this year, but next year I think I'll just play basketball with my friends.

Realize that your teen may need more than one conversation before reaching a resolution. If your teen wants to talk late at night, be sure to schedule another time to continue the conversation if you are too tired. If your teen cries, it's a sign that he feels emotionally safe with you. Continue to listen without stopping the tears.

It is never too late to improve your listening skills and repair your relationship with your teen. He will appreciate your efforts and gradually begin to share more of his problems and feelings with you.

Tip 72

Communicate your own feelings and needs.

While teenagers often complain that their parents don't know how to listen, parents frequently complain that their teens don't listen to *them*. If your teen doesn't listen to you, it's probably because of the way you speak to her. Even the most sensitive, intuitive adults don't always know how to communicate effectively.

Thomas Gordon coined the term "I-message" in his groundbreaking book, *Parent Effectiveness Training*. He distinguished "I-messages," which communicate your own feelings and needs, from "You-messages," which describe your child, often in negative terms.

Compare the following "I-messages" and "You-messages":

"You-message" (incorrect): "You always leave your dirty dishes on the table. Can't you clean up after yourself?"

"I-message" (correct): "When you leave your dirty dishes on the table, I feel resentful because it gives me extra work to do."

"You-message" (incorrect): "You're so inconsiderate when you turn the volume up so loud. Don't you know that you're the only one around here who likes that music?"

"I-message" (correct): "When you turn the music up so loud, I feel frustrated because I can't concentrate on my writing."

The problem with "You-messages" is that they make your teen feel accused and invalidated, and they create an adversarial relationship. If you can remember to focus on your own feelings and needs instead of finding fault with your child, your statements will be less threatening to her, and she will be more likely to listen to you and work cooperatively to find a solution to the problem. Using I-messages forces us to figure out exactly what's going on with ourselves. Although sometimes difficult to do, this introspection is necessary for finding mutually agreeable solutions to conflicts.

Many other authors have described a similar way of communicating feelings and needs. In his book *Compassionate Communication,* Marshall Rosenberg recommends adding a specific request to the basic "I-message." In the first example above, the parent could make the following request after the I-message: "Would you be willing to put your dirty dishes in the kitchen sink after eating?"

If you can remember to communicate clearly your own feelings and needs, you will build a relationship with your teen based on trust and respect rather than on criticism and control. This open communication will be a vital factor in your teen's drug resilience.

Tip 73

Solve conflicts democratically.

All families have conflicts. The mark of a healthy family is not the absence of conflicts but the manner in which the conflicts are resolved. If you try to change your teen's behavior with punitive consequences such as grounding him, decreasing his allowance, not letting him watch TV, or giving him extra chores, he will become resentful and angry, and he may rebel. Rewards are not much better because even if you manage to attain superficial compliance, you will have no guarantee that your teen has acquired any deeper values, such as respect for others.

Adolescents are less likely to use drugs when their parents use discussions and joint decision making to solve conflicts with them, rather than authoritarian, punitive approaches to discipline. With a democratic approach to discipline, you will create an atmosphere of respect and trust, and your teen will have nothing to rebel against.

If you have not yet begun holding family meetings, now is the time to start. (See Tip 47.) They can be a helpful first step in switching to a more democratic approach to discipline. Don't be surprised if your teen is suspicious at first. He might think that family meetings are a new trick to get him to do what you want.

I recommend using the first few meetings to discuss pleasant or neutral topics, such as where to spend the summer holidays. After your teen understands the process, you can introduce the idea of discussing conflicts. Put a sheet of paper on your refrigerator, and encourage your children to write down problems they have with each other or with you. Then discuss those problems at the next family meeting. After you have accomplished these goals, your teen will understand that meetings are beneficial, and you can then begin to put your *own* conflicts on the agenda. For example, if your teen has a drum set and the noise bothers you, write this problem on the agenda and discuss it at the next family meeting.

When discussing conflicts, be sure to use I-messages to state your feelings and needs, and listen well when your teen responds with his own feelings and needs. (See Tips 71 and 72.) Try to reach consensus before implementing a solution. If your teen does not abide by the solution during the week, there is no need to nag. Instead, simply put the item on the agenda again.

Be sure to discuss only those conflicts for which you can give a convincing I-message. If your teen's behavior does not interfere with your own needs in any tangible way, then you are probably not dealing with a conflict of *needs* but rather a conflict of *values*. For example, if your teen plays his drum set instead of doing his homework, that is a conflict of values. (See the next tip for ways of dealing with conflicts of values.)

Tip 74

Deal wisely with conflicts of values.

When trying to change your teen's behavior, it is important to understand the difference between conflicts of needs and conflicts of values. When your teen's behavior bothers you but *does not have a direct, tangible effect on you,* then you are dealing with a conflict of *values* rather than a conflict of *needs.*

Examples of conflicts of values are: .

- Your son does not eat salad.
- Your daughter dyes her hair green.
- Your son doesn't do his homework.
- Your daughter's room is messy.
- Your son wears jeans with holes in them.
- Your daughter has a friend who smokes.
- Your son does not share your religious faith.

Conflict-resolution techniques and family meetings are not an effective way to address these conflicts of values because you cannot give a convincing "I-message" (a statement of how your child's behavior interferes with your own needs). Your teen will probably tell you, "It's none of your business," and she's absolutely correct because she should have the right to make choices that affect her personally.

Even though a direct approach does not work well for these conflicts of values, you can use other, indirect approaches to change your child's behavior. The following influencing techniques can be quite effective.

- Model your own values, but don't impose them on your child.
- Offer interest, encouragement, and support. For example, if your son procrastinates about doing homework, ask him what he is learning in school. Offer to help quiz him for an upcoming test.
- Give information. For example, inform your teen about good nutrition.
- Discuss the issue nonjudgmentally and ask for your teen's point of view. For example, ask your teen to share other people's reactions to her green hair.
- Share your own childhood experiences, if appropriate. For example, if you had a friend with a bad influence on you, describe this experience and explain how you found other friends.
- Let natural consequences occur (but don't create artificial ones). For example, your daughter may eventually have trouble finding things if she never cleans up her room.

By encouraging, but not forcing, your teen to change her personal values, you will gain her trust and respect, and she will be more likely to adopt your values as her own. This will be especially important when she must make decisions about drugs.

When dealing with conflicts of any kind with your teen, remember this important paradox: *The less you try to control your children (with punishments or rewards), the greater will be your positive influence on them, and therefore the greater your ability to change their behavior.*

Tip 75

Come to a mutual agreement about curfews.

Curfews are often a source of conflict and tension with teenagers because parents make the mistake of imposing them in an authoritarian way and punishing teens when they do not arrive home at the designated time. This approach makes teens feel resentful and overly controlled and can lead to rebellion.

It is possible to come to a mutual agreement about curfews without imposing any kind of negative consequences (punishment). The key to accomplishing this is to understand the major purpose of curfews, which is to keep your teen safe and to know when you should start to worry.

You can explain to your teen that it is your job to keep him safe. Explain the possible dangers about being out later than a specific time. If you are worried about your teen getting enough sleep, discuss your concerns with him. However, the choice about when to go to bed is ultimately his to make because that is a personal value. He might have to learn the hard way. But whatever your concerns, it is important to share them with your teen.

After sharing your concerns, you can come to a mutual agreement about curfews. When my children were teenagers, I would ask them where they were going and when I could expect them to be home. If they said, "I'll be home around midnight," we would make the agreement that they would call me if their plans changed. I felt comfortable with that arrangement because it met my need to know when I should start to worry. My children were very respectful of my need for reassurance. They always came home by the time we had agreed on, or they called to let me know if they would be late.

Sometimes teens actually *request* a curfew because it helps them "save face" with their friends and resist peer pressure to stay out late. It's much easier for a teen to say, "My mom told me to be home by midnight," than to say, "I want to leave now." With the latter statement, the friends might put pressure on him to stay longer. A parental curfew gives a teen an excuse to leave, which his peers can understand. When my children told me, "Just tell me when I have to be home," I gave them a reasonable curfew with the understanding that they could use that as a pretext to leave a social situation.

Your teen also deserves to know where *you* are at all times and when he can expect *you* to be home, so be sure to give him this information. With a mutual agreement about curfews, you will have no need for the use of punishment, and your teen will have no reason to rebel. This respect for curfews will help to keep your teen safe and drug free.

Tip 76

Encourage healthy risks.

Many teenagers like to take risks in order to try out their skills, measure themselves against others, conquer fear, and see how far they can go. Teenagers with low self-esteem might take risks to prove to others how brave they are, in hopes of increasing their popularity. In addition to these needs and desires, many teenagers, especially those who have never had a serious illness or accident, have a sense of invulnerability. They feel strong and healthy, and they don't fully understand the dangers involved in what they do. Peer pressure also enters into risk-taking behavior. This pressure to conform may lead teenagers to make unwise choices in order to feel included in a group. An additional factor is that some teens are naturally higher risk takers or sensation seekers than others because of an inherited temperament trait. These various factors can lead to dangerous behaviors, such as experimenting with drugs or sex or driving recklessly.

You can minimize the likelihood of dangerous behavior by encouraging your teen to take healthy risks instead of dangerous ones. If your teen feels the need to be physically challenged, you might suggest activities such as rock climbing, wilderness camping, white-water canoeing, diving lessons, or ropes courses. If your teen participates in these activities with experienced instructors and guides, there is very little danger. The benefit is that your teen will be able to "flirt with danger" safely, conquer fear, build self-confidence, make friends, and get some exercise.

If your teen wants to compete against others in a safe way, you can suggest that she try out for a sports team, participate in a music competition, or audition for a play. If she wants intellectual challenges, you can encourage her to participate in a math contest, join a debate team, or take advanced classes while still in high school. The risk in these challenging and competitive activities is that there is the possibility of failure, so these, too, are a way of "flirting with danger." Be sure to encourage activities that are of interest to your teen and that provide the right amount of challenge.

If your teen should fail a test or lose a competition, allow her to express feelings of sadness or disappointment. Try to be a good listener, and avoid giving advice about what she could have done better. Remind her that she was courageous to try, and ask her what she learned from the experience. Encourage her to try again.

By encouraging healthy physical and intellectual risks, you will help your teen meet her need to see how far she can go, while avoiding the dangers associated with inappropriate, risky behaviors.

Tip 77

Introduce your teen to spiritual practices.

Drugs are alluring because they can create a temporary sense of awe and euphoria, which mimics a spiritual experience. However, drugs are deceptive because they replace the inner work that adolescents need to do to build a meaningful faith. During adolescence, teens begin to ponder the "big," spiritual questions, such as "Why am I here?", "What is the meaning of life?", "How should I spend my time before I die?", "Is the universe a friendly place?", and "Where does evil come from?"

To find meaning and purpose in life, we need to have faith in something, whether we call it God, the power of love, the wisdom of nature, the inherent goodness of human beings, or simply a vision for a better world. One of the tasks of adolescence is to find a belief or ideal that gives hope and also provides a context for answering the "big" questions. Teens who have been raised within a specific religious faith often begin to question the ready-made answers that they have been taught. This is a sign of healthy growth.

It is only natural that you will want your child to adopt whatever faith has nourished you, and it is important to share your personal beliefs and spiritual practices with your child. However, making religious worship mandatory will probably only lead to rebellion, or at the most, superficial compliance. In fact, your teen may be *more* likely to adopt your faith if you refrain from forcing it on him. So try to be supportive and open-minded as your teen finds his own spiritual path.

Throughout the centuries, people have used a variety of spiritual practices to center themselves and feel connected to whatever they have faith in. These practices include prayer, meditation, yoga, walking in nature, special diets, poetry, singing, chanting, and dancing. Don't be afraid if your teen wants to learn about spiritual practices that differ from yours. Keep in mind that dancing or climbing a mountain can be spiritual practices, which help your teen feel connected to other people or to nature.

You can make use of teachable moments to help your teen think about the "big" questions. For example, when the topic of terrorism comes up in the news, ask your teen to share his theories about the causes of terrorism. If a friend or family member is dying with dignity and has found meaning and purpose in life, let your teen talk with him.

By allowing your teen to explore spiritual practices, he will find ways to connect to whatever he believes to be good and true. This will help to inoculate him against the seductive power of drugs.

A word of caution: Teach your teen to be extremely wary of cults with charismatic leaders who promise spiritual "enlightenment" in exchange for large sums of money, or who encourage followers to take drugs or engage in sex, violence, or self-mutilation. Doomsday and satanic cults are especially dangerous.

Tip 78

Encourage your teen to do something to improve the world.

When discussing sources of stress for teens, very few books mention the fact that teens can be deeply affected by the state of the world. Many teenagers are troubled by terrorism and war, the disappearing rain forests, or the starving children, and they, like adults, often feel powerless to make the world a better place. With all the terrorist attacks and natural disasters in recent years, some teens even wonder if the world as they know it will still exist when they grow up.

These feelings of discouragement and pessimism for their own future can lead to chronic anxiety and tension, thereby increasing their risk of getting involved with drugs. Sometimes drug use is simply an attempt to escape from all the unpleasantness and uncertainty of life, including the dismal state of the world.

Teens don't often talk about these pessimistic feelings, possibly because they don't want to sound silly. Or maybe they don't want to burden the adults in their lives. But even if your teen doesn't talk about these issues, it is likely that she thinks about them.

You can counter feelings of discouragement or powerlessness by encouraging your teen to get involved in volunteer work that helps to improve the world. Even if your teen is not discouraged about the state of the world, this kind of work can boost her self-esteem by making her feel that she is helping to make the world a better place.

Volunteer activities will be more meaningful to your teen if they are related to her personal interests. If your daughter likes animals, she might want to get involved in a fund-raising project to save the chimpanzees in Africa. If your son enjoys working with children, perhaps he would find it personally rewarding to volunteer at a shelter for refugees or homeless families. Or if your teen is interested in politics, you could steer her in the direction of helping with an election campaign for a political candidate who shares her values.

To encourage your teen, tell her about young people who have made a difference in their communities or in the world. Recently, there was an inspiring story in the news about a teenager who started a Boy Scout troop for fatherless boys living in poverty. Stories like that will reassure your teen that, with determination and perseverance, one person *can* make a difference and that there is no need to become apathetic. Even if your own family has limited financial resources, you can empower your teen to help others.

Tip 79

Help your teen feel physically attractive.

Teenagers' self-esteem is closely tied to how attractive they feel. Those who think they do not fit the cultural norm of slimness or beauty are at risk for taking drugs to mask their feelings of inferiority and to feel accepted by a group. As already mentioned, overweight teens (especially girls) often begin to use certain drugs to curb their appetite so they can lose weight.

There are several steps you can take to enhance your teen's self-image about her body.

- *Exercise and diet.* A healthy body enhances physical attractiveness, so encourage your teen to get plenty of outdoor exercise and to eat wholesome foods. Be a good role model by exercising regularly and eating wisely. Serve plenty of vegetables and fruit, and keep junk food out of your home.
- *Acne treatment.* Many teens are deeply embarrassed by pimples. Don't hesitate to bring your teen to a dermatologist. There are now effective treatments for this common ailment, including dietary changes and medicated skin creams.
- *Clothing.* Teens feel that it is important to conform to current clothing styles, whether it's bell-bottom pants, faded blue jeans, tight-fitting skirts, or baggy T-shirts. Even teens with high self-esteem find it difficult to resist the pressure to conform. If you cannot afford to buy stylish new clothes for your teen, encourage her to earn the money, make her own clothes, exchange clothes with

friends, or shop at a second-hand clothing store. Help your teen to be resourceful, and don't shame her for wanting new clothes.

- *Orthodontia.* If your child has crooked teeth, orthodontia is definitely worth the cost if you can afford it. In fact, I personally consider orthodontia to be a valid medical expense, rather than a luxury. But don't sacrifice your own financial needs to the point of becoming resentful, and don't make her feel guilty for the money you spend to have her teeth straightened.

- *Contact lenses.* If your child needs to wear corrective lenses, contact lenses can greatly enhance her attractiveness and self-esteem. If there is an extra expense involved, try to reach a financial arrangement with which you both feel comfortable.

- *Media awareness about beauty-enhancing products and services.* Discuss cultural stereotypes of beauty with your teen, and remind her that the people who promote beauty-enhancing products and services, such as hair dyes and cosmetic surgery, are in business to make a profit. You don't want her to feel that she must radically change her appearance to be attractive. Help your teen learn to value her unique facial features, skin and hair color, and body proportions.

Tip 80

Don't underestimate the impact of racial stereotypes.

No matter what color your child's skin is, others will make assumptions about him based on his race. If your child belongs to a racial minority, these assumptions will be particularly harmful because they will be part of the pattern of oppression of that race. If he is your biological child, you will be prepared for this because you grew up with racism. If your child is adopted and has a different skin color from yours, you may not know what to expect.

Racial stereotypes hurt children because they prevent people from seeing the children as individuals. In the case of drug abuse and addiction, for example, there is an assumption in the United States that drug abuse is more prevalent among poor African American youth than among affluent European American youth. However, there is actually a greater percentage of rich white teenagers who abuse drugs, although they are not as likely to end up in the juvenile justice system because their parents can afford to bail them out of jail, hire expensive lawyers, and send them to private residential treatment programs. Drug abuse affects every race, ethnic group, and socioeconomic class, with the only difference being that children from poor families (regardless of skin color) are more likely to become drug dealers to support their habit.

Even positive stereotypes can be harmful. For example, black people in the United States have a reputation for excelling at sports such as basketball. But it is a mistake to assume that every tall black teen will be interested in basketball. This assumption based on racial stereotyping could prevent his teachers from recognizing his potential for science or creative writing.

Racial stereotyping can also lead to discrimination, teasing, criticism, and physical assault. It is sad, but true, that people hurt others simply because of their skin color. Similar stereotyping and discrimination can occur between different ethnic groups even though the groups have the same skin color.

Racial and ethnic stereotyping are highly stressful for children of all ages, and stress can be at the root of anxiety, depression, and substance abuse. During adolescence, it is especially painful for teens to feel different from others, because their self-esteem is directly related to feelings of belonging and acceptance. So try to be aware of how racist attitudes might be affecting your teen on a daily basis, and be supportive by listening well and taking his side if he describes a painful experience. Don't ever imply that discrimination occurred because of something he did. He needs you to be his unconditional ally.

Tip 81

Be aware of the higher risk of drug abuse among homosexual teens.

A person cannot control his sexual orientation any more than his eye color. The discovery of one's homosexual orientation can occur as early as nine or ten years of age, and it often comes with shock, terror, confusion, and shame. The cause of these feelings is not the homosexuality itself but rather the child's awareness of the cultural stigma and oppressive attitudes toward homosexuals. Not surprisingly, gay and lesbian adolescents are at high risk for substance abuse, depression, and suicide.

Nobody knows what causes homosexuality, but it is clear that inappropriate parenting is *not* the cause. So if your child turns out to be gay, lesbian, or bisexual, realize that there is nothing you could have done to change his sexual orientation.

Homosexual adolescents often hide their sexual orientation from their friends and families, pretending to be heterosexual so they will be accepted. They are terrified that others will discover the truth, so they make huge efforts to convince others (and perhaps also themselves) that they are heterosexual. They may even joke about gays and lesbians. However, constantly lying and pretending to be what they are not can take a toll on their mental health.

Those who feel brave enough to openly admit their homosexuality are also under considerable stress because they risk becoming targets of stereotyping, teasing, discrimination, and even violence. Whether they admit their homosexuality or not, the constant stress felt by gay and lesbian teens can lead to substance abuse in an attempt to feel accepted by their peers, control their anxiety, and relax in social situations. Drugs can be their way of coping in an intolerant world.

Your attitude is of utmost importance. Whether you know that your child is homosexual or not, it is wise to express tolerance toward homosexuals and avoid negative remarks or jokes about them. Welcome gay and lesbian people into your life. Explain to your child that the stereotypes are false and that the oppression of homosexuals is harmful. For example, it is not true that there is a greater percentage of pedophiles among homosexuals than among heterosexuals.

A supportive, tolerant attitude toward homosexuals will help your child feel more comfortable with his sexual orientation if he is gay. Although his life will probably still be difficult because of the cultural intolerance of homosexuality, at least he will have you as a supportive ally. Even if he does not reveal his sexual orientation to you, he will understand that you will not reject him if he were to tell you that he is gay.

If you were taught that homosexuality is immoral, it will be understandably difficult for you to become tolerant of gay people. However, by doing so, you may help prevent your gay teen from using drugs or committing suicide. Even if your child is not gay, he will learn from your example to be tolerant and supportive of others who are gay.

Tip 82

Identify sources of family stress.

I know a family whose fifteen-year-old son began experimenting with drugs when his mother's cancer, which had been in
remission for five years, suddenly took a turn for the worse.
The parents failed to see any connection between this major
family stress and their son's behavior. Instead, they implemented stricter supervision and discipline. Needless to say,
this approach didn't work, and they eventually sent their son
to a strict private boarding school. Unfortunately, the mother
died several years later. It saddens me that she and her son
were not able to enjoy a close, loving relationship during her
last years of life.

There is always a reason why teens turn to drugs, and this
reason is often some form of stress. Family stresses include the
illness or death of a family member, parental substance abuse,
domestic violence, divorce, remarriage, new siblings (through
birth, adoption, or remarriage), legal problems, financial problems, poverty, and moving to a new location. The common ele-
ment in all of these family stresses is that the parents are
understandably preoccupied with their own problems and have
very little attention or patience for the children.

Another obvious stress for teens is physical or sexual abuse.
However, it's possible to live in a nonabusive, seemingly loving
home and still feel alienated, unloved, or misunderstood.
Teens can feel stressed if there is unresolved sibling rivalry or
if the parents are frequently angry or depressed, use punitive
discipline, or simply don't spend enough time with the children. A common but frequently overlooked source of stress is

simmering resentment by a parent (often the mother) who has sacrificed her own needs excessively. I often see this problem in the mothers who consult with me.

Take some time to identify the sources of stress in your family, from your teen's point of view, and write them down. You could even do this exercise together as a family. Then think about whether everyone's needs are being met. If not, what can you do to change the situation? Consider the option of family therapy or individual therapy for yourself. Your child may also benefit from individual therapy.

In the above example, I wish the parents had gone to a family therapist when their son first showed signs of getting in trouble with drugs. Everyone in the family could have expressed their fear about the mother's illness, and perhaps they could have cried together. The boy would have felt understood, supported, and connected. Instead, he had to deal with his terror alone, and the only relief he could find was through drugs.

By identifying and addressing possible sources of stress in your family, you will take an important step in preventing your teen from turning to drugs in order to cope.

Tip 83

Identify sources of school stress.

In addition to family stress, school stress can be a major contributing factor to drug use by teens. This source of stress is often overlooked or underestimated.

Possible sources of school stress include inappropriate teaching methods, harsh discipline, boring classes, overcrowded classrooms, conflicts with teachers or peers, being teased or excluded, bullying, violence, racist or sexist oppression, embarrassing incidents, exposure to drugs, difficult or boring homework, parental pressure for academic excellence, the teen's own perfectionism, and high-stake exams.

Most of these sources of stress are beyond your control. However, you can check into all of the educational options for your child. Often, a city has more than one kind of high school. Perhaps there is another one that better meets your teen's interests, learning style, or need for individual attention. You can also take your child out of school and homeschool if it is legal where you live.

The principal of your teen's school needs to know if your child has been the victim of violence, if drugs are being sold at school, or if a teacher has used inappropriate discipline or made a racist remark. Encourage your teen to discuss these problems with the principal, or tell the principal yourself if your teen agrees.

You can support your teen at home by listening to him complain about school. If he claims that a teacher was unfair, give him your unconditional support even though you might disagree with him. Instead of trying to defend the teacher, listen to him attentively while he vents his anger. Later, he may come to see his teacher's point of view.

If your teen is struggling in his classes or seems to have ongoing problems with one or more of his teachers, arrange a meeting with his teachers. They may have observations and insights to help you better understand your child and the situation. Sometimes the problem stems from family stress rather than directly from school stress. Realize, too, that it could be an indication of drug use.

If the problem lies with only one or two school subjects, you can help him learn those subjects at home or find a tutor for him. If you have expertise in a subject that your teen is struggling with, such as a foreign language, by all means share your knowledge and help. Your job is not to *make* your child do his homework, nor should you do it for him, but you can support and help him.

Even if you can't change the sources of school stress, your unconditional support, interest, and involvement will help your teen cope with school stress without resorting to drugs.

Tip 84

Teach your teen stress-management skills.

Drug abuse is more likely to occur when teens feel stressed. In the previous two tips I described possible sources of stress at home and at school. Additional sources of stress can result from living in poverty or in unsafe neighborhoods, threats of terrorist attacks, and war. Don't underestimate lesser forms of stress, including sexual maturation, falling in love, feeling different, finding a job, lack of free time, or moving to a new home or school. Realize that many teens are stressed much of the time.

You cannot avoid all stress in your child's life. However, you can help your teen learn to cope with stress in healthy ways by teaching her the following four stress-management skills.

- *Body awareness and relaxation skills.* The first step is to help your teen recognize *when* she is stressed. Teach her to pay attention to her body signals, such as insomnia, fatigue, inability to concentrate, depression, irritability, or anxiety. Show her how to relax by breathing deeply, stretching, resting, or taking a hot bath. If you practice a form of meditation, teach it to your teen. Give her a shoulder massage.

- *Identifying the source of stress.* The next step is to find the source of stress and figure out what to do about it. For example, if she begins to have trouble sleeping after starting a new job, it might be wise for her to work fewer hours or reduce time spent on other activities.

- *Time management.* Many teens feel overwhelmed by their various activities and feel that they never have enough time. Time management is a useful skill to teach your teen. When my children felt overwhelmed by a major homework project, I helped them divide up the project into manageable mini-steps, and I gave them a large calendar on which to write down what they needed to accomplish each day. With this clear schedule in front of them, the project no longer seemed so daunting. They knew exactly what they had to accomplish each day in order to complete the project on time.

- *Emotional release.* Encourage your teen to talk about what's bothering her and refrain from giving her advice so she can freely vent her feelings. Allow her to cry if she needs to (and if she feels safe enough). If your teen finds it hard to discuss certain topics with you, ask her if she would feel more comfortable talking with another person, such as a religious leader, youth group leader, teacher, school counselor, psychologist, or a close friend or relative. Let her know that there is a whole community of caring people available to help her with her problems.

Tip 85

Look for signs of depression.

Teens who suffer from depression are at high risk for abusing drugs to enhance their mood. Although teens might feel better temporarily when they use drugs, emotional problems almost always worsen with prolonged drug use. Keep in mind, too, that repeated drug use can actually *cause* anxiety or depression, so it can become a vicious cycle.

Symptoms of depression in teenagers include:

- Lethargy, fatigue, excessive sleeping (however, remember that teens need a lot of sleep)
- Persistent sadness
- Insomnia
- Loss of appetite or overeating
- Feelings of hopelessness, worthlessness, or self-reproach
- Lack of interest in friends, school, or family activities
- Restlessness, irritability
- Difficulty concentrating or making decisions
- Self-mutilation or talk of suicide (if your child is suicidal, get *immediate* help)

If you think that your teen is depressed, don't hesitate to seek professional advice. It's better to err on the side of caution than to wait until something tragic happens. You can say to your child, "You seem to be pretty sad lately, and you've complained of insomnia. I've also noticed that you've lost interest in your friends. Is something bothering you? Is there anything I can do to help?" If he shrugs you off and says that everything is fine, you can say, "I'm worried about you. Would you be willing to see a doctor or a psychologist?"

There are several reasons why your child may feel more comfortable talking with a professional rather than with you. Perhaps he feels guilty or depressed about something that he is embarrassed to reveal, such as a sexual encounter. Perhaps he wants to protect you from knowing how bad things really are for him. Maybe he is worried that you will feel guilty, blame him, give unwanted advice, or be unable to help. If he welcomes the opportunity to talk to a professional, be sure it is someone who is compassionate and nonjudgmental, who can listen well, and who has experience with adolescent emotional problems.

A medical evaluation is advisable, but be wary of antidepressants, which may only mask the problem, and which have not been proven to be safe or effective during adolescence. Fortunately, there are effective psychotherapeutic approaches for depression. Even if you think your child has inherited a predisposition to depression, realize that environmental factors, such as stress or emotional trauma, always play a role.

Physical exercise, social support networks, and emotional expression can help counteract depression. So encourage your teen to exercise regularly and stay connected to other people. As always, be sure to listen well when he shares his feelings with you, and encourage him to cry if he needs to.

By addressing your teen's depression and other serious emotional problems as soon as you notice them, you will be taking an important step in keeping him away from drugs.

Tip 86

Support drug prevention efforts in your city.

You can play an indirect but important role in helping your child grow up drug free by working with other parents to expand your influence in your community. When all parts of a community work together to create a drug-free world for adolescents, they reinforce and support the message that you want your child to learn. There are several ways you can help to accomplish this goal.

- Work with your teen's school to encourage drug-prevention educational programs if the school does not already have these. It is a good idea for schools to have some form of these programs every year, preferably beginning at the age of ten, whether it's a class taught by a credentialed teacher, an educational film, or a guest speaker. Effective speakers can include former alcoholics or drug addicts, law enforcement officers, psychologists, health workers, and substance abuse counselors. Effective preventive programs emphasize the dangers of drugs and ways to resist social pressures to use them.
- Work with your teen's school to establish a strict policy about drug use on school grounds, as well as a comprehensive identification and referral program for students who have problems with drugs. Help to establish a drug advisory committee if your teen's school does not have one.
- Work with your community to establish after-school recreational activities for adolescents. For example, the city I live in finally built a skateboard park after parents

complained for years that there was not much for teens to do. Swimming pools, bowling alleys, basketball courts, tennis courts, and skating rinks can all help to keep teens out of trouble. Help to establish drug-free places for dancing or listening to music.

- Help to establish alcohol-free and drug-free social events in your community, including dances, parties, and rock concerts. Patronize smoke-free and alcohol-free restaurants in your city.
- Support the efforts of law enforcement personnel, and teach your teen to respect them.
- Vote for legislators who will adequately fund community substance abuse prevention and treatment programs. Get involved in fund-raising efforts to support these important programs.
- Vote for legislators who will adequately fund programs that strengthen and support families, such as health care, day care, and educational opportunities for families with limited financial resources.
- If you belong to a religious community, work to establish a faith-based substance abuse prevention program.

Tip 87

Share information about drugs through "teachable moments."

Instead of having long, serious talks about drugs, it is more effective with teenagers to make use of times when the topic
arises naturally. Think of these opportunities as "teachable moments," when you can give your teen information and share
your values.

If a famous athlete has been using steroids, discuss this with
your teen and explain the dangers involved in using steroids to
enhance one's muscle strength. Inform yourself about steroids,
and tell your teen exactly what it does to the body. If there is
an alcohol-related car accident in your city, you can seize this
opportunity to point out to your teen the dangers of driving
under the influence. In our city, a high school teacher was arrested for growing and selling marijuana. If something like this
happens in your city, you can point it out to your teen and
show him that selling illegal drugs is extremely risky and can
destroy a person's career.

Don't hide family secrets from your teen if these can help
him learn about the dangers of drugs. If Uncle Joe was an alcoholic, and if this addiction ruined his life, tell your teen
about Uncle Joe and show him photos. Explain that he was a
gifted student, but he started drinking and couldn't kick the
habit. If Great Aunt Emily was a smoker and later died of lung
cancer, tell your teen how sad you felt that she died at such a
young age. You can also share your own past experiences with
drugs if you feel comfortable doing so and if you think your
teen will benefit from hearing about them. These personal sto-

ries will mean much more to your teen than impersonal lectures about the dangers of tobacco or alcohol.

When you discuss these topics with your teen, your attitude is important. If you sound like you are preaching or moralizing, your teen will not want to listen. Below are examples of a wrong way and a right way to talk to your teen.

Wrong: "Did you hear about those kids who got killed while driving under the influence? That's what could happen to you if you're not careful. I hope you never do anything that stupid."

Right: "I felt so sad when I read about those kids who were killed in the car accident yesterday. They had their whole lives before them. They probably had no idea how risky it was to drive under the influence. It makes me angry that nobody told them how dangerous it was. Their parents must be absolutely devastated. How does it make you feel?"

By sharing your personal feelings, your teen will not become defensive, and by inviting your teen to share his thoughts, you will encourage further discussion. He might even feel comfortable telling you about someone he knows who drinks and drives. This could lead to a useful discussion about how to refuse a ride with an intoxicated driver.

Tip 88

Teach your teen about addiction and the brain.

It is important for your teen to have a basic understanding of what drugs do to the brain. The following is a brief summary of the information that your child should know.

Whether drugs are swallowed, inhaled, snorted, or injected, they enter the bloodstream and reach the brain, where they produce pleasurable effects such as euphoria, relaxation, alertness, or reduction in anxiety. These effects are called a "rush" or a "high."

What's wrong with wanting to feel good? Teens often ask this question when someone tries to convince them to stop using drugs. Tell your teen that drugs can permanently damage parts of the brain involved in learning and memory, as well as other parts of the body. Another problem is that most psychoactive drugs are addictive, and the mechanism of addiction is basically the same for all of them. Addictive drugs stimulate a pleasure center in the brain called the nucleus accumbens by increasing the available amount of dopamine (a neurotransmitter). Whenever this part of the brain is stimulated, people feel a strong urge to repeat whatever they did to stimulate that part of the brain.

But why is addiction so bad? What's wrong with taking a drug repeatedly? The problem comes from the fact that *the brain naturally adapts to the drug and compensates for its presence.* When this occurs, two things can happen. First, the drug loses its potency, so the person must take larger quantities of it to experience the same "high." This is called developing tolerance to the drug. Second, without the drug, the person will feel *worse* than she did before she took the drug. The symptoms of withdrawal can be both physical (such as headaches or nausea) and psychological (such as depression or anxiety) and can be extremely unpleasant.

Eventually, the person continues to take the drug not so much to feel good but *to avoid feeling bad.* The craving for the drug will dominate her life and become more important than eating, going to school, or spending time with family and friends. When an addicted person stops using a drug, it can take months for the brain to regain the ability to feel relaxation or pleasure without it. Sometimes the brain never returns to normal. Some people continue to crave alcohol or cocaine years after they stop using it.

Tolerance can happen very quickly. Many teens report that their first experience with a drug was the best. The high never feels quite as good as it did the first time. Yet they continue to take the drug in hopes of recapturing that initial experience and also to avoid the withdrawal effects, which inevitably become worse with continued use. Contrary to popular opinion, marijuana is addictive, although the withdrawal effects are not as dramatic as with some of the other drugs.

With this information about drugs, addiction, and the brain, your teen will be less likely to experiment with drugs.

Tip 89

Explain why drug use is especially risky during adolescence.

Even if you enjoy wine with your dinner or take tranquilizers to help you sleep, you can be very clear, without being hypocritical, about the dangers of drug and alcohol use by your teen. Explain that you are an adult and that you use these substances responsibly. Provide your teen with the following information on why drugs and alcohol are especially risky during adolescence.

1.   Drug use during adolescence can permanently damage the brain. Children's brains develop rapidly during adolescence, and drugs can stunt brain growth or cause permanent damage, leading to long-term problems with learning, memory, logical reasoning, mood, and personality.

2.   The risk of illness and death from drug use is greater during adolescence. An obvious danger is the risk of driving while intoxicated, which is even greater for inexperienced drivers. Adolescents may not be aware of the dangers of overdosing or combining drugs, and they may not know that a single dose of certain drugs can be deadly. Another danger is contracting HIV or hepatitis C by sharing needles for injecting drugs. The earlier a person begins to smoke tobacco, the greater his chances are of getting lung cancer and cardiovascular disease later on. Drug withdrawal symptoms during the vulnerable adolescent years can increase a teen's chance of committing suicide.

3.   Drug use can increase the risk of unprotected or unwanted sex, resulting in pregnancy, sexually transmitted

diseases, and rape trauma. Drugs can reduce a person's inhibitions and make boys become sexually aggressive or violent. Drugs can lower a girl's resistance to sexual advances or even make her unconscious ("date rape" drugs). Adolescents are inexperienced and therefore more vulnerable to these risks.

4. Drug use during adolescence can mask problems and prevent normal psychological development. For example, if a boy always drinks alcohol or smokes marijuana to relax during social situations, he will not acquire the social skills he will need later in life.

5. Adolescents are more vulnerable to addiction because of their immature brains, sense of invulnerability, and sensitivity to peer pressure. Furthermore, they do not understand the nature of addiction; they may think that their withdrawal symptoms are a case of the flu, or blame others for making them feel depressed. Teens who are dependent on drugs think that they can stop any time they want, that it's simply a matter of choice. Studies have shown that the age of a first alcoholic drink is an important factor in predicting alcohol dependence. Those who do not consume any alcohol until they are young adults are much less likely to become addicted.

6. Using illegal drugs is a crime and can result in serious problems with the law. Being arrested can have a more devastating impact on a teen's life than on an adult's life because it can damage a teen's chances of completing his education and finding employment.

Tip 90

Describe how drugs can affect your teen's appearance.

For many teens, warnings of dire future health problems do not have as much of an impact as do the more immediate disadvantages of using drugs. Because of the importance of conforming to group norms for appearance during adolescence, teens are likely to avoid anything that detracts from their attractiveness. Therefore, in addition to telling your teen about the major dangers and health problems caused by drugs, be sure to mention also the more immediate, observable effects caused by various drugs.

A brochure to discourage teen girls from smoking states, "When's the last time you saw a model with stained teeth, dirt-brown fingers and smoke coming out of her nose on the cover of a magazine?" Another sentence asserts, "Kissing a smoker is like licking an ashtray." These statements are likely to have a strong impact on teenage girls.

Photos are also an effective teaching tool. An article in a popular U.S. weekly news magazine showed two photos of the same woman, one taken before she began using methamphetamine, the other taken after one year of continued use. She looked as if she had aged by ten years. If you come across any photos like those, show them to your teen.

Give your teen the following information on how specific drugs can affect appearance.

- Nicotine: bad breath, cigarette odor on clothing, stained teeth, brown fingers
- Alcohol: bad breath, vomiting, slurred speech

- Marijuana: dry mouth with lips sticking to teeth, chapped lips, bloodshot eyes
- Inhalants: bad breath, runny nose, red or watery eyes, rash or sores around nose and mouth, slurred speech, vomiting
- Methamphetamine: skin sores and scabs ("crank sores" caused by scratching imaginary bugs under the skin), dark circles under the eyes, bad breath, tooth decay
- LSD: trembling hands and limbs
- Ecstasy: clenched jaw, clenched hands, acne-like rash
- Cocaine: bad breath, dry mouth and lips
- Heroin: skin flushing or itching
- Ritalin: tremors, vomiting

Tip 91

Role-play imaginary scenarios involving drugs.

Saying "no" to drugs is easier for teens when they have a wide variety of responses at their fingertips. Role-playing imaginary situations can be a valuable teaching tool. You can take turns playing the various roles in the following list of situations that your teen might encounter.

Scenarios

- You are at a friend's home, and your friend says, "My parents aren't home, and there's an open can of beer in the fridge. Let's taste it."
- You are with a small group of friends at school during a break between classes, and one of them says, "My older sister gave me a joint (marijuana cigarette). Let's smoke it after school."
- You complain to a friend that you feel overwhelmed by all the homework you have to do, and he offers you one of his prescription Ritalin tablets, saying, "Ritalin really helps me concentrate. Try it. Maybe it will help you too."
- You are at a party and your friends are taking methamphetamine. They offer you some, saying, "You'll feel better than you've ever felt in your entire life. It's unbelievable. Why don't you start with a really small amount?"
- You are at a party and you notice some people in a back room doing something with a white powdery substance.
- Your friend has been drinking alcohol at a party and is obviously intoxicated. You depend on her to drive you home in her car.

Ten Ways to Refuse Drugs

- Simply refuse: "No thank you." "I'm not interested." "I don't smoke pot."
- Change the subject or suggest another activity: "Let's go play basketball." "Have you seen the new movie that's playing in town?"
- Blame your parents: "My parents would kill me if they found out."
- Find a valid excuse: "I want my brain to be clear for an important math test tomorrow."
- Say why you don't need drugs: "No thanks. I'm feeling pretty good already."
- Share your family history of addiction: "My grandmother was an alcoholic, and I know it can be hereditary. I'm afraid I won't be able to stop once I start." "I don't want to die of lung cancer like my uncle."
- Use a medical reason: "I'm taking medication that would make it risky for me to use that drug."
- Describe your temperament: "No thanks. I'm not a risk taker."
- Share other personal reasons: "I'm trying to be a good role model for my little brother."
- Find a pretext to walk away: "No thanks. I just remembered that I'm supposed to meet a friend at 5 o'clock."

Tip 92

Be alert for signs of drug use.

There are many possible signs of drug use in teens. Some of them are:

- Change in sleep habits (insomnia or excessive sleep)
- Change in eating habits (loss of appetite or sudden binge eating)
- Sudden weight loss
- Change in school performance, unexplained absences, or disruptive behavior at school
- Change in friends or loss of interest in extracurricular activities
- Change in clothing habits, poor hygiene
- Anxiety, panic attacks, mood swings
- Listlessness, apathy, lack of energy
- Unusual hyperactivity, alertness, fidgeting, agitation
- Anger, hostility, violent outbursts
- Perceivable physical symptoms (bloodshot eyes, skin sores, rash, shaky hands, staggering gait, chronic cough, slurred speech, nose bleeds, dry mouth)
- Complaints of nausea, constipation, diarrhea, headaches, chills, sweating
- Secretiveness, lying, withdrawal from family activities
- Money problems (missing cash, depleted savings account)
- Frequent use of products to mask drug use (eye drops, breath fresheners, incense)
- Smell of drugs on breath or clothing (alcohol, tobacco, marijuana, inhalants)

- Presence of drugs or drug paraphernalia in room

These signs can be indications of drug use. However, only the last two are strong indicators by themselves, so don't over-react if your child has some of the other symptoms. If you notice any of the above physical symptoms, first take your teen to a doctor for a medical check-up, because the symptoms could be caused by an illness or allergy.

There are also many possible explanations for a change in friends. Perhaps your teen has joined a new club at school or a sports team and finds that she has more in common with those people than she does with her former friends. On the other hand, you don't want to overlook signs that might indicate that your child is experimenting with drugs. If your teen suddenly begins to drop old friends for no apparent reason and starts doing activities with teens who encourage her to skip school or stay out late at night, you should be concerned.

Likewise, a sudden drop in grades is a possible indication of drug use, but there are other possible causes. Your child may be taking classes that are too difficult, or perhaps she finds it difficult to study because of family stresses. Be aware, however, that good grades do not necessarily imply that your teen is staying away from drugs. Some teens can continue to function at a high level in spite of their involvement with drugs. Additionally, some manage to keep their grades up by using stimulants as study aids.

With knowledge of the possible signs of drug use, you will be able to intervene early if your teen begins using drugs.

Tip 93

Avoid five major mistakes if your child has tried drugs.

If you suspect that your child has begun to experiment with drugs, there are five things to avoid doing.

1. Don't overreact. Drug experimentation does not imply drug dependence. Although you may have strong feelings of anger, terror, or guilt, try to maintain a sense of perspective. If your child has tried smoking marijuana, for example, it would be unreasonable to send him to a treatment program immediately. However, if your teen has experimented with an especially dangerous drug, you should take immediate action.

2. Don't attempt to control your child's behavior with punitive discipline. When your teen begins to experiment with drugs, you may think that you have been too permissive. However, becoming more strict and controlling is likely to have the opposite effect of what you intend because your teen will have more incentive to rebel and conceal his behavior from you to avoid getting caught.

3. Don't try to protect your child from the natural consequences of his drug use. This would be the beginning of "enabling," which means facilitating a person's drug use by protecting him from the natural consequences of his behavior. An example of enabling a teen's drug use is making false excuses to your child's teachers or employers about his absences from school or work. It is better for your teen to be forced to confront an angry boss during his early stages of drug use than end up in jail or in

the hospital after prolonged and dangerous use, which you have facilitated through your enabling behaviors.

4. Don't condemn your teen's behavior with moralistic lectures. If you tell your teen that drugs are immoral or that he is a bad or weak person for trying them, he will probably walk away or become angry. Or he may listen politely but continue using drugs.

5. Don't ignore the problem. A common mistake is to assume that a child's drug experimentation is just a passing phase and that he will outgrow it. Although this may be true in many cases, you should not ignore the fact that your child has begun to experiment with drugs. Some parents let obvious drug use pass without mentioning it because they want to appear "cool." That attitude will not help your child deal with the confusing and dangerous world of drugs.

So what should you do instead? See the next two tips for suggestions of intervention strategies.

Tip 94

Confront your teen lovingly if you suspect occasional drug use.

If you suspect that your child has begun to experiment with drugs, it is essential that you discuss the topic with her. Choose a moment when you are both relaxed and in a comfortable location. The car is not a good place because your child will feel trapped. Be calm and supportive. Begin with your observations and worries without accusing your child. Here's an example of how you can bring up the topic: "I saw some cigarette papers in your pants pocket when I washed them, and I thought you might be using them to roll marijuana joints. I'm concerned about this. Would you be willing to discuss this with me?"

If you have a good relationship with your teen, she will not be afraid to answer you honestly. In fact, she may be relieved that the topic is finally out in the open because most teens are not comfortable keeping secrets from their parents. Together, you and your teen can then address the reasons for her drug experimentation. It may simply be curiosity or peer pressure. On the other hand, her drug use may reflect a deeper problem such as school or family stress, a romantic disappointment, depression, or anxiety.

If your relationship with your teen is already strained, she will probably deny any drug use, accuse you of snooping, tell you it's none of your business, or storm out of the room. If this occurs, you can say, "Are you afraid I might punish you? Are you feeling the need for your privacy to be respected?" Also, continue sharing your own feelings: "I'm disappointed that you do not wish to discuss this with me because I am concerned and I want to help you. I'm not trying to control you, and I won't punish you. Let's discuss this again another time." *Do not give up.* Bring up the topic again at a later time.

Meanwhile, try implementing some of the other tips in this chapter, and don't underestimate your importance in your child's life. Research has shown that increased parental involvement with young adolescents (eleven to fifteen years of age) who have begun to drink alcohol can actually prevent the drinking behavior from progressing.

Be aware that teens who are already addicted often lie about their drug use. If your teen's drug use continues in spite of your best efforts to discuss it with her or to improve your relationship with her, it is still not too late to help her, but you will benefit from additional resources. Inform yourself about intervention and treatment approaches (see Resources), or seek the advice of a substance abuse counselor or psychologist. See also the next tip in this book.

A word of caution: If your teen has experimented with an especially dangerous drug (such as crack cocaine), you will need to take more immediate action.

Tip 95

If your teen regularly abuses drugs, convince him to get treatment.

Most addicted teens think they can stop using drugs any time, and they often resist treatment because they consider their drug use to be a personal choice, similar to becoming a vegetarian. They think that the conflict with their parents is simply one of different values, and they do not understand how their behavior affects their parents.

It is true that drug use begins as a conflict of values between teens and parents. (See Tip 74.) However, because of the damaging effects of drugs, continued use soon becomes a conflict of needs. An effective intervention strategy, therefore, is to tell your teen, directly but lovingly, *how his behavior affects you in specific, concrete ways.* Here are some examples.

- Your need for your child to survive and thrive: "I love you, and it frightens me to see you destroying yourself with drugs. I would be devastated if you had an accident or died."
- Your need for financial security: "When you continue to use illegal drugs, I worry that I might have to bail you out of jail some day."
- Your need for connection: "I felt sad when you didn't show up at our family picnic. When our whole family is together, it meets my need for connection."
- Your need for dependable help: "When you forgot to put out the trash yesterday, I felt disappointed and resentful because it gave me extra work when I was tired."

- Your need for respect: "I felt hurt and frustrated when you yelled at me yesterday. I'd like us to be able to talk to each other respectfully."

A more formal intervention strategy is to arrange a meeting with your teen and your entire extended family, a few of your teen's close friends, and perhaps your teen's employer, a sports coach, or a teacher. Each participant, in turn, confronts the teen lovingly by giving specific examples of ways that the teen's drug use has personally affected that person.

Follow up all of your interventions with an urge for treatment: "I see a connection between this problem and your drug use." Then explain the nature of addiction and ask your teen, "Would you be willing to get treatment?" Be prepared at that point to offer your child several treatment options from which to choose. If he resists treatment but promises to stay drug free, let him try. If he is addicted, he will probably have a relapse. Repeat your interventions until your child realizes that he needs help.

In some cases a teen's denial and resistance to treatment are so strong that school-mandated or court-mandated treatment may be necessary. Be sure to join a support group to get support from other parents who have struggled with their children's substance abuse.

Chapter 6

Ages 18 to 25

Tip 96

Prepare your child to expect alcohol and drugs on college campuses.

When your child leaves home, it is only natural to feel anxious about how she will cope away from home. You will not be able to supervise your child or have any control over her at all. This is a frightening thought for many parents. You will need to trust that she has the security, information, self-esteem, and self-discipline that she will need to resist drugs.

If your teen is planning to leave home to attend college, it is important to prepare her for the reality of college life, because she is likely to be offered drugs and alcohol in student dormitories or apartments. Even if you have been using a democratic approach to discipline, as described in this book, your child will almost certainly meet young people who have been raised with power-based, punitive methods of control and who do not know how to handle freedom. When these young people leave home, they rebel by engaging in all the activities that were forbidden when they lived at home, such as trying drugs, engaging in sexual activities, staying up late, and procrastinating in their studies. Their parents' strict discipline has prevented them from becoming self-disciplined and self-regulated. Your child will need your support when she meets these young people who have challenges to overcome as they learn to handle freedom wisely.

Let your teen know that alcohol consumption is common on most college campuses and universities. Other drugs, such as methamphetamine and marijuana, are also easily available, and synthetic drugs such as Ecstasy are popular among older teens and young adults. To avoid being pressured to take these substances, suggest that your teen try to meet other students who do not drink alcohol or take drugs. Perhaps she can join a club or become involved in volunteer activities to meet other students who share her interest for drug-free activities.

Be sure to warn your teen about the practice of concealing drugs in foods or drinks, and warn your daughter about date rape drugs. These tasteless, odorless drugs can be put into a drink, and they cause the person to fall into a deep sleep. Tell her not to accept any drink from an already opened container, including nonalcoholic ones, and never to leave a drink unattended, even to go to the bathroom. It is safest for a girl to pour her own drink from an unopened container.

You can role-play various social situations to prepare your son or daughter for possible encounters with drugs or alcohol away from home. Create imaginary scenarios and encourage your teen to have fun finding ways to refuse drugs. This playful approach will help to alleviate some of the anxiety you both may be feeling about the impending separation.

By warning your teen about possible encounters with drugs on college campuses, you will prepare her for these unpleasant realities of college life.

Tip 97

Don't pressure your child to pursue a specific career.

When your child was born, you probably had career dreams for him, which you may still have. Perhaps you hope he will become a doctor, lawyer, or musician. Maybe you want him to follow in your own footsteps or go into a career that you would have liked to pursue. However, it's time to give up those dreams because your child needs to make his own choices.

Young people who feel pressured by their parents to pursue a specific career might begin their studies with that goal in mind, only to discover that it doesn't inspire them. They are then faced with a dilemma because they want to please their parents but also want to be true to themselves. I have met young people whose parents threatened to withdraw their financial support if their son or daughter did not pursue the parents' choice of career. This rigid attitude puts tremendous stress and pressure on young people at an age when life is already stressful for them. In a study examining alcohol consumption in college students (age eighteen and older), students who felt pressured and who perceived a lack of choices in their life were more likely to drink in order to cope with stress.

It is common for young adults to change career directions as they try different fields of study or work. A certain job might sound appealing to them, but then seem boring after a few months or years. Most people learn best by doing, so they must actually experience something before they can determine if they like it. This vacillating is perfectly normal and is not a waste of time. Your child will learn something from each experience and will get to know himself better. Don't be afraid to encourage your child to try different careers. Because of the rapid changes brought about by information technologies, career options are changing rapidly, and the trend nowadays is for people to have more than one career during their lifetime. In fact, some of the jobs your son or daughter will have in the future may not even exist yet.

Try to avoid putting pressure on your child to pursue a specific career. If he is making progress toward a university degree, be glad he is doing something productive, and continue to support him even if it is not the career you had in mind. Try to be understanding even if he decides to quit his studies. Some young people benefit from taking a year off to work or travel. Even if he decides not to continue his education, your emotional support and relaxed trust in your child will allow him to find his career path without stress or pressure.

Tip 98

Keep in touch when your child leaves home.

When your child has moved away from home, be sure to keep in touch. Even though she is independent and lives somewhere else, you are still her parent, and she will benefit from an ongoing connection with you, which will strengthen and sustain her during difficult times.

Here are some suggestions for keeping in touch with your adult child:

- Send e-mail messages, cards, letters, and occasional presents to your adult child. Don't underestimate the importance of these gestures of your love, even if it's only a one-line e-mail to say "Hi."
- Call your adult child on the phone, but don't be intrusive. Sometimes it is better to let her know ahead of time (perhaps by e-mail) on what days you will have the time to talk, and then let her take the initiative to call if she wishes.
- Don't worry too much about lack of phone calls or e-mail. Your son or daughter may be busy studying or may prefer to spend time with friends rather than have long conversations with you.
- When you talk on the phone, show an interest in your adult child's studies, work, and social life. Don't probe, but ask specific questions to follow up on past information she has given you. For example, "Did you get into the choir you auditioned for?" Or, "How did the job interview go on Tuesday?" She will be pleased that you remembered

those details. Often, the most helpful thing you can do is simply to listen.

- Don't give unwanted advice. A good guideline is to avoid giving any advice unless your son or daughter specifically asks for it. If you do not impose advice, your adult child will be more likely to seek your advice.

- Don't ever forget your adult child's birthday. A card or a small present is better than an e-mail greeting because a concrete object will give your child a tangible reminder of her connection to you.

- In addition to news about your own life, keep your adult child up to date about family and neighborhood news. Let her know how grandpa's health is and which cousins got married. Tell her which of your family friends and neighbors have died, gotten divorced, moved away, or had a baby. If you run into a former teacher or friend of your child, relay the discussion to her.

- Organize occasional family reunions with extended family members. Don't wait for a wedding or a death to bring the family together.

- Propose family trips. Don't assume that your adult child is too old to spend the holidays or travel with you. Suggest activities to do together as a family, but don't be too upset if she has other plans.

Tip 99

Make your adult child's home visits pleasant.

If your child has moved away from home, be sure to welcome him warmly whenever he returns for a visit. Try to make his home visits pleasant, no matter how much stress there is in your life. These are not the times to burden your son or daughter with your own problems.

You can help your adult child maintain a sense of connection and security by serving foods you know he likes and continuing to honor the family traditions you established when he was younger, such as birthdays or special holiday celebrations. Don't ever assume that your child is too old for these. Although he may not ask for them, he will probably be pleased that you continue the rituals.

It is pleasant for many young adults when they return home to find their old books and games, so don't get rid of these items without consulting your son or daughter. After my children left home, they did not let me give away their stuffed animals and games. These objects were like a symbolic connection to their childhood. Now I am glad I have these toys for my grandchild!

Another way of making your child's home visits pleasant is to avoid criticizing him or giving unwanted advice. If you find his hairstyle, clothing, or food preferences strange, it is best to keep your opinion to yourself because it's really none of your business.

If your family changes through divorce, death, or a move to a new home after your child leaves home, be alert for signs of depression in your child, and be especially attentive to maintaining family traditions to help him maintain a sense of continuity and security. Keep familiar decorations on your walls, and maintain photo albums documenting your family's history.

Some parents are so delighted when their adult child visits home that they become his servant. However, the risk of doing too much for your child when he visits is that you might become resentful, and he will sense this. It is perfectly appropriate to expect him to help around the home. You may even have some special projects for him to assist you with, which make use of his physical strength or knowledge. These requests will help your child feel useful. However, avoid burdening him with too many responsibilities, or he may not want to visit you any more!

With an ongoing, stable connection with you and with the home of his youth, your son or daughter will feel renewed and strengthened each time he visits you. He will feel that he has roots from which to go forth into the world, and this foundation of security will give him the courage to face life's challenges with confidence. The more solid this foundation and his connection to it, the less he will need drugs to cope with life's inevitable ups and downs.

Tip 100

A final word of encouragement.

A mother once said to me, "My son is twenty-one years old, and I've made all the mistakes. Is it too late to help him?" My answer was, "Absolutely not. With information and support, you can help your son."

Children are complex, even at birth, and parenting is one of the hardest jobs in the world. Our culture does not recognize or reward adequately the important work that parents do, and many parents are forced to choose between their own needs and those of their children. Single and low-income parents understandably have an especially difficult time meeting their children's needs. Parents are often blamed for their children's problems, but are rarely trained for the job or given adequate support.

Try not to be too hard on yourself if your child is troubled or uses drugs, even if you think that the problem results from your own past mistakes. You have always done your best with the information and resources available to you. Remember, too, that you are not the only influence on your child. Many other factors, some beyond your control, have played a role in determining the kind of person your child has become. But whether you or other causes have contributed to your child's problems, the important thing to know is that *you can always be part of the solution.*

The most important theme running throughout this book is that *meaningful connection* can both prevent and heal behavioral and emotional problems. So look for ways to stay connected to your child as she grows or to reconnect with her if she has problems or has become emotionally distant from you. Your child desperately wants to feel connected to you and the family, and she will welcome your attempts to re-establish a loving relationship, even though you may feel that she is pushing you away at first. It may take time and numerous attempts for her to trust you and begin to feel a sense of connection again. Above all, get the support you need, and don't ever give up.

Resources

Scientific References

The information in this book is based on numerous scientific research studies. Please see the author's Web site at www.awareparenting.com/drugfreekids/references.pdf for a list of these references.

Recommended Books for Parents (General)

Aldort, Naomi. *Raising Our Children, Raising Ourselves*. Bothell, Wash.: Book Publishers Network, 2006.

Armstrong, Thomas. *In Their Own Way: Discovering and Encouraging Your Child's Multiple Intelligences*. New York: Jeremy P. Tarcher/Putnam, 2000.

Aron, Elaine. *The Highly Sensitive Child*. New York: Broadway Books, 2002.

Breeding, John. *The Wildest Colts Make the Best Horses: What to Do When Your Child Is Labeled a Problem by the School*. Austin, Tex.: George Weir, 2003.

Breggin, Peter. *Reclaiming Our Children: A Healing Plan for a Nation in Crisis*. New York: Da Capo Press, 2000.

———. *The Ritalin Fact Book: What Your Doctor Won't Tell You About ADHD and Stimulant Drugs*. New York: Da Capo Press, 2002.

Cohen, Larry. *Playful Parenting*. New York: Ballantine Books, 2001.

Faber, Adele, and Elaine Mazlish. *How to Talk So Kids Will Listen and Listen So Kids Will Talk*. New York: Harper Collins, 1999.

———. *How to Talk So Teens Will Listen and Listen So Teens Will Talk*. New York: Harper Collins, 2005.

Gordon, Thomas. *Parent Effectiveness Training*. New York: Three Rivers Press, 2000.

Kohn, Alfie. *Unconditional Parenting: Moving From Rewards and Punishments to Love and Reason.* New York: Atria Books, 2005.

Leo, Pam. *Connection Parenting: Parenting Through Connection Instead of Coercion, Through Love Instead of Fear.* Deadwood, Ore.: Wyatt-MacKenzie Publishing, 2005.

Luvmour, Sambhava, and Josette Luvmour. *Everyone Wins: Cooperative Games and Activities.* Gabriola Island, B.C.: New Society Publishers, 1990.

Miles, Karen. *Psychology Today: The Power of Loving Discipline.* Indianapolis, Ind.: Alpha Books, 2006.

O'Mara, Peggy. *Natural Family Living: The Mothering Magazine Guide to Parenting.* New York: Pocket Books, 2000.

Pipher, Mary. *Reviving Ophelia: Saving the Selves of Adolescent Girls.* New York: Riverhead Books, 2005.

Pollock, William. *Real Boys: Rescuing Our Sons from the Myths of Boyhood.* New York: Owl Books, 1999.

Rosenberg, Marshall. *Nonviolent Communication.* Encinitas, Calif.: Puddle Dancer Press, 2003.

Samalin, Nancy. *Loving Your Child Is not Enough: Positive Discipline That Works.* New York: Penguin, 1998.

Solter, Aletha. *Helping Young Children Flourish.* Goleta, Calif.: Shining Star Press, 1989.

_____. *Tears and Tantrums: What to Do When Babies and Children Cry.* Goleta, Calif.: Shining Star Press, 1998.

_____. *The Aware Baby,* revised edition. Goleta, Calif.: Shining Star Press, 2001.

Sweet, Win, and Bill Sweet. *Living Joyfully with Children.* Atlanta: Acropolis Books, 1997.

Books for Parents About Drugs

Some of these books recommend an authoritarian (punitive) approach to parenting, which is not consistent with the approach described in *Raising Drug-Free Kids.* They are nevertheless included here because of the valuable information they contain about drugs and treatment methods.

Abraham, Henry David. *What's a Parent to Do? Straight Talk on Drugs and Alcohol.* Far Hills, N.J.: New Horizon Press, 2004.

Besseling, Renee. *Parents: A Natural Preventive Against Drugs.* Troy, Mich.: Performance Resource Press, 2004.

Biddulph, Stephen. *Alcohol: What's a Parent to Believe?* Center City, Minn.: Hazelden, 2003.

Cermak, Timmen L. *Marijuana: What's a Parent to Believe?* Center City, Minn.: Hazelden, 2003.

Cohen, Peter. *Helping Your Chemically Dependent Teenager Recover: A Guide for Parents and Other Concerned Adults.* Center City, Minn.: Hazelden, 1998.

Falkowski, Carol. *Dangerous Drugs: An Easy-to-Use Reference for Parents and Professionals.* Center City, Minn.: Hazelden, 2003.

Hillin, Harvey, and Mary Hillin. *Drugs and Youth: What Parents, Teachers, or Helping Professionals Should Know.* Bloomington, Ind.: Authorhouse, 2005.

How to Tell When Kids Are in Trouble with Alcohol/Drugs. Center City, Minn.: Johnson Institute/Hazelden, 1998.

Jewell, Roger H., and Lauro Amezcua-Patino. *What You Should Know and Are Afraid to Ask: Drugs Among Children and Adolescents—A Parent's Guide.* Frederick, Md.: Publish America, 2004.

Ketcham, Katherine, and Nicholas A. Pace. *Teens Under the Influence: The Truth About Kids, Alcohol, and Other Drugs—How to Recognize the Problem and What to Do About It.* New York: Ballantine Books, 2003.

Kuhn, Cynthia, Scott Swartzwelder, and Wilkie Wilson. *Just Say Know: Talking with Kids About Drugs and Alcohol.* New York: Norton, 2002.

Leibrock, Norman. *Parents, Help Your Child Say No to Drugs.* Philadelphia: Xlibris, 2002.

Maxwell, Ruth. *Kids, Alcohol and Drugs: A Parents' Guide.* New York: Ballantine Books, 1991.

Milhorn, H. Thomas. *Drug and Alcohol Abuse: The Authoritative Guide for Parents, Teachers, and Counselors.* New York: Da Capo Press, 2003.

Schwebel, Robert. *Saying No Is Not Enough: Helping Your Kids Make Wise Decisions About Alcohol, Tobacco, and Other Drugs—A Guide for Parents of Children Ages 3 Through 19.* New York: Newmarket Press, 1998.

Simonelli, Frank, Jr. *Drugproof Kids: The Ultimate Prevention Handbook for Parents to Protect Children from Addictions.* Los Angeles: Tre Publishing, 2004.

Somdahl, Gary L. *Drugs and Kids: How Parents Can Keep Them Apart.* Salem, Ore.: Dimi Press, 1996.

Books for Children About Drugs

Ages 5 to 8

Hastings, Jill, and Marion Typpo. *An Elephant in the Living Room.* Center City, Minn.: Hazelden, 1994.

Super, Gretchen. *Drugs and Our World*. Fairfield, Iowa: 21st Century Books, 1997.

Vigna, Judith. *My Big Sister Takes Drugs*. Morton Grove, Ill.: Albert Whitman & Co., 1995.

Ages 8 to 12

Friedman, David P. *Focus on Drugs and the Brain*. Jefferson City, Mo.: Troll Communications, 1991.

Gottfried, Ted. *The Facts About Alcohol*. Salt Lake City, Utah: Benchmark Books, 2004.

Landau, Elaine. *Cigarettes*. London: Franklin Watts, 2003.

_____. *Alcohol*. London: Franklin Watts, 2003.

_____. *Cocaine*. London: Franklin Watts, 2003.

Levert, Suzanne. *The Facts About Steroids*. Salt Lake City, Utah: Benchmark Books, 2004.

Menhard, Francha R. *The Facts About Inhalants*. Salt Lake City, Utah: Benchmark Books, 2004.

Taylor, Clark. *The House That Crack Built*. San Francisco: Chronicle Books, 1992.

Ages 10 to 18

The Drug Abuse Prevention Library. This series of easy-to-read, illustrated books (by various authors) is published by the Rosen Publishing Group (New York). It includes books about specific drugs, such as *Crack, Heroin, Marijuana*, etc., as well as titles about drugs in general, such as *Drugs and Stress, Drugs and Denial, Drugs and Violent Crime, Drugs and Your Brain, Drugs and AIDS*.

Drugs: The Straight Facts. This series of books is published by Chelsea House (New York). It includes the following titles (by various authors): *Alcohol, Antidepressants, Body Enhancement Products, Cocaine, Date Rape Drugs, Designer Drugs, Diet Pills, Ecstasy, Hallucinogens, Heroin, Inhalants, Marijuana, Morphine, Nicotine, Prescription Pain Relievers, Ritalin and Other Methylphenidate-Containing Drugs, Sleep Aids*.

Hyde, Margaret. *Alcohol 101: An Overview for Teens*. Fairfield, Iowa: 21st Century, 1999.

Masline, Shelagh Ryan. *Drug Abuse and Teens: A Hot Issue*. Berkeley Heights, N.J.: Enslow Publishers, 2000.

Mezinski, Pierre, and Melissa Daly. *Drugs Explained: The Real Deal on Alcohol, Pot, Ecstasy, and More*. New York: Harry N. Abrams, 2004.

Packer, Alex J. *Highs! Over 150 Ways to Feel Really, Really Good Without Alcohol or Other Drugs.* Minneapolis: Free Spirit Publishing, 2000.
Sheen, Barbara. *Teen Alcoholism.* San Diego: Lucent Books, 2004.
Smith, Miriam. *Addiction: The "High" That Brings You Down.* Berkeley Heights, N.J.: Enslow Publishing, 1997.
White, Tom. *Bill W.: A Different Kind of Hero: The Story of Alcoholics Anonymous.* Honesdale, Penn.: Boyds Mills Press, 2003.

Organizations and Web Sites

Addiction Technology Transfer Center: www.nattc.org (816-482-1200)
Adult Children of Alcoholics: www.adultchildren.org (310-534-1815)
Al-Anon/Alateen: www.al-anon.org (888-425-2666)
Alcoholics Anonymous (AA): www.aa.org (212-870-3400)
American Council for Drug Education: www.acde.org (800-488-3784)
Association of Recovery Schools (ARS): www.recoveryschools.org (615-248-8206)
Co-Anon Family Groups: www.co-anon.org (800-898-9985)
Cocaine Anonymous: www.ca.org (310-559-5833)
Families Anonymous: www.familiesanonymous.org (800-736-9805)
Hazelden Foundation: www.hazelden.org (800-257-7810)
Join Together Online: www.jointogether.org (617-437-1500)
Mothers Against Drunk Driving (MADD): www.madd.org (800-438-6233)
National Clearinghouse for Alcohol and Drug Information: www.health.org (Part of the U.S. Department of Health & Human Services: 800-729-6686)
National Council on Alcoholism and Drug Dependence: www.ncadd.org (800-622-2255)
National Inhalant Prevention Coalition (NIPC): www.inhalants.org (800-269-4237)
National Institute on Alcohol Abuse and Alcoholism (NIAAA): www.niaaa.nih.gov (Part of the U.S. Department of Health & Human Services: 800-729-6686)
National Institute on Drug Abuse (NIDA): www.nida.nih.gov (Part of the U.S. Department of Health & Human Services: 800-729-6686)
Narcotics Anonymous: www.na.org (818-773-9999)
National Association for Children of Alcoholics: www.nacoa.org (301-468-0987, 888-554-2627)
Office of National Drug Control Policy: www.whitehousedrugpolicy.gov (Drug policy information clearinghouse: 800-666-3332)

Resources

Office of Safe and Drug-Free Schools: www.ed.gov/about/offices/list/osdfs
   (Part of the U.S. Department of Education: 800-624-0100)
Parents: The Anti-Drug: www.theantidrug.com (800-729-6686)
Partnership for a Drug-Free America: www.drugfree.org (212-922-1560)
Secular Organizations for Sobriety/Save Our Selves (SOS International):
   www.sossobriety.org (323-666-4295)
Students Against Destructive Decisions (SADD): www.saddonline.com
   (877-723-3462)
Substance Abuse and Mental Health Services Administration (SAMHSA):
   www.samhsa.gov (800-273-8255)

Acknowledgments

I would like to express my gratitude to all the people who have helped with this book, especially my son, Nick Solter, his wife, Sonja Solter, and my husband, Ken Solter, who all encouraged me to write it and who gave me valuable feedback on the manuscript. I would also like to thank the three other parents who took time out of their busy schedules to read the manuscript and provide me with detailed, insightful suggestions for improvement: Melanie Jacobson, Jim Pearson, and Kristen Rohm.

These acknowledgments would be incomplete without mentioning the other authors, too numerous to list, who have been my mentors without even knowing it. Many of their books are listed in the Resources section. I am especially indebted to the late Thomas Gordon, Ph.D., whose work gave me the courage to raise my own children with gentle discipline. Finally, I am appreciative of the scientific researchers in the fields of child development and substance abuse who continually further our knowledge about these complex issues.

About the Author

Aletha Solter, Ph.D., is a Swiss American developmental psychologist, workshop leader, and consultant. She is the founder and director of the Aware Parenting Institute (www.awareparenting.com), an international organization with certified instructors in twelve countries.

Dr. Solter earned a master's degree in human biology at the University of Geneva, Switzerland, where her studies included a two-year course with the Swiss psychologist Dr. Jean Piaget. She then completed a doctoral degree in psychology at the University of California, Santa Barbara. She currently resides in Goleta, California, and is the mother of two grown children.

Her three other books (*The Aware Baby, Helping Young Children Flourish,* and *Tears and Tantrums*) have been translated into many languages, and she is recognized internationally as an expert on emotional development and nonpunitive discipline.

Dr. Solter is available for lectures, workshops, and phone consultations. She can be reached at solter@awareparenting.com. Her Web site is www.awareparenting.com.